THE ROAD TO STATION X

Sarah Baring

SAPERE
BOOKS

THE ROAD TO
STATION X

Published by Sapere Books.

20 Windermere Drive, Leeds, England, LS17 7UZ,
United Kingdom

saperebooks.com

ISBN: 978-1-80055-059-9.

To my sons William Astor and Edward Baring, and for Osla Henniker-Major who shared all our wartime work, and who I think would have enjoyed this story of it.

TABLE OF CONTENTS

IN GERMANY — 1937

When I was seventeen my parents sent me to Munich in Germany for further education and to learn the language. I was green and unsophisticated, tall and skinny with wavy hair the colour of rich mouse. I had long gangly legs which I kept tripping over and which resulted in them being liberally decorated with bits of sticking plaster to cover the grazes.

I went reluctantly and with bad grace because I really wanted to go to Italy. My innocent mind was full of fantasies of romantic Italian boys, but my mother dismissed them as unsuitable for my tender age and I was dispatched to Germany forthwith.

I was installed in the home of a Graf and Gräfin who were both kind and welcoming. I was forced to learn German because they pretended not to be able to speak English. Every morning an elderly lady of obviously reduced means came to help me struggle through the grammar and the extraordinary structure of sentences with the verb at the end.

The afternoons were spent at art school where I studied illustrative lettering with great joy. I was taken to the opera twice a week but, as I was tone-deaf to anything other than jazz, it was not much fun; and to sit through *The Ring* was a form of torture. I was embarrassed by my lack of culture in the musical arts, but being a visual person I was at least rewarded by the splendid architecture and the flamboyant baroque decoration.

I began to notice that food was very scarce, butter and such things as marmalade were almost non-existent. The Gräfin did her best under the circumstances and fed me and the two other resident English girls with a reasonably decent diet.

But something else was terribly wrong. There was tension in the air and an atmosphere of fear pervaded the city. The citizens seemed to shrink away from anyone in uniform and hesitate to voice an opinion even to their family and friends. The culprit was, of course, the Nazi Party who were predominant in the district; they strutted about like roosters in a barnyard causing young and old to quail at the sight of them.

In Munich, during the summer of 1937, an odious anti-Jewish newspaper was published called *Die Juden*. It was both vicious and destructive and nobody bought it. As a result of this public rejection, the powers that be in the Reichstag decreed that it should be prominently displayed, framed, covered with glass and erected on the railings of nearly every street corner. Myself and other like-minded English girls also studying the language were outraged by this obscenity and the seventeen-year-old energy was detonated by the unjust and atrocious persecution of the Jewish people.

After a period of reflection followed by frustration, the mischievous elasticity of the teenage mind gave birth to a crusade, the consequence of which forced me to return to England in disgrace some months later, still rebellious and self-righteous nevertheless.

At the beginning of our campaign against the Nazis, we satisfied ourselves with the sport of circling the Odeonsplatz in the city centre and refusing to raise the right arm in a statutory salute to Hitler, thereby tormenting the Gestapo who didn't dare arrest us because we were foreigners, but we soon tired of that.

Next on the agenda was visiting the Charlton Tea Rooms, regularly frequented by Hitler and his gang of assassins. We would choose a table as close as possible and stare at them in obvious distaste. It was a pretty senseless occupation because I do not think they noticed us, but it gave us vicarious pleasure and a good opportunity to observe them.

Adolf Hitler was usually dressed entirely in grey, giving the impression of a haunting spectre with black piercing eyes that drilled into you. His hair was carefully brushed obliquely across his forehead, but despite the intimidating appearance the effect was rather comical. Field Marshal Goering, on the other hand, favoured an all-white uniform with medals and decorations hung on every spare inch of his tunic and he was so fat that his bloated stomach bulged over the tablecloth. Goebbels and Streicher, the Jew baiters, defied description other than to say they looked sub-human and specimens of evil ectoplasm. We eventually decided that these visits were a waste of time and money and that something more serious and significant had to be done to display our hatred of the regime. I think the exposures of the newspaper distressed us the most and that was where our vendetta should be directed.

The plan, hardly a plot, was to secure a hammer, sneak out at night, smash the glass and tear down the offensive publication from its frame. The only hurdle to overcome was the suspicions of the Graf and Gräfin's younger son, who was a dedicated member of the Hitler-Jugend. They were like Nazi Boy Scouts and wrapped in their cause. He might betray us, or even worse, his gentle parents. To ensure that he fell into a deep sleep we doped his evening ersatz coffee with four crushed aspirins.

The stage was set nearby in Durchstrasse, the scene a street corner. We struck the glass in the middle of the frame, pulled down and tore up the filthy newspaper and moved on to the next target.

That was when the fun began, the noise had alerted the S.S. and the chase was on. Now, a Stormtrooper with baton and jackboots can be an alarming sight, but thus equipped they cannot run, at least not fast enough. Their clatter made an excellent danger signal, but to round a corner and bump into one unexpectedly involved a spectacular turn of foot made easier by wearing an old pair of gym shoes.

After a few nights of this hedonistic action, the glass was suddenly replaced by wire mesh which was a slight hindrance, but overcome by purchasing a pair of wire cutters from an ironmonger in another district; this process of removal took longer and scouts had to be posted at intervals. In the end, of course, we were caught, giving grounds for embarrassment to our Foreign Office — who were trying to be congenial to the Germans — and sent home in disrepute.

I was in some fear and trepidation as to my mother's reaction, but all she said was "Well done, despite your nuisance value I hope you learnt the language."

DEBUTANTE

In 1938, these were the words I heard as I walked into the room for my first deb dance. "Well, look what's happened to little Sarah Norton!" Trying to gather my wits and hide my fright, I looked up and standing there before me were five white-tied, tail-coated males. At first I did not recognise them, but after a few seconds and through the disguise of sartorial excellence I perceived my childhood friends.

What a metamorphosis! A picture flashed through my mind, indelibly printed, of scruffy, tousle-haired boys who had teased me mercilessly but allowed me to join them in a game of rounders. My only problem, which made me cry, was that I was unable to pee up the garden wall like they did. I didn't understand why and went sobbing to Nanny, who said she would explain when I got older. My mother's friends had produced mostly males and although at the time I craved for the company of girls to play with, my male-dominated world was to stand me in good stead in the future. I must have looked a bit different from the tangled tomboy I used to be, but all flowers have a bud which eventually comes out, which was what I was supposed to be doing.

"Coming out" and being a debutante had never given me much food for thought as I was only interested in horses, but my mother told me I was to be presented at Court that year and that I would have to learn to curtsey properly, none of that bob up and down stuff so admired by the Edwardians to illustrate good manners to their elders and betters.

I was dispatched off to Miss Vacani's, a celebrated school of dancing and deportment. I had attended her dancing classes

13

many years before where we were taught to mince across the floor smiling prettily, and point the toe nicely. Due to my innate clumsiness I could do neither, so despite the beauty of my frock and the matching double-satin ribbons in my hair, much to Nanny's chagrin, Miss Vacani suggested that the lessons should be suspended until I was older.

So the years went by and I found myself back in Knightsbridge at the dancing emporium. I thought this curtseying business was going to be a doddle. I fancied myself as a gymnast and could do the splits with ease. I had practised this particular exercise for years because it was the one thing the boys could not do.

Miss Vacani eyed us up and down; there were at least fifteen girls in the class. I hoped she hadn't remembered my childish ineptitude. "Now, my darlings, stand up straight, heads high, poise is most important." I felt a perfect idiot parading round amongst the other girls, who were going through the same drill and feeling equally foolish. Another command addressed to me: "Sarah Norton, don't look at your feet. They are meant to move, not be gazed at, darling."

This supposedly easy obeisance to the King and Queen was actually profoundly difficult. You had to bring your left leg behind your right leg, bend the knee almost down to the floor keeping your head high and eyes straight forward. Going down was not too bad, but coming up was almost impossible without wobbling. Such an error Miss Vacani would not countenance. It took hours of practice to become perfect and I am not sure I ever got it right, but at least I got rid of the wobble.

Then there followed a series of fittings at the dressmakers for my court dress. Mine was made of ivory satin, cut straight with a small train and puff sleeves. I hated it, but no amount of sulking and remonstrations that it was unfashionable would change my mother's mind. The style made it difficult to do the curtsey and whip the train round with my heel on completion of the manoeuvre.

The day of my presentation at Court arrived and early on a hairdresser fixed the three white Prince of Wales' feathers firmly to the back of my head for this important occasion. My mother looked beautiful in white silk with her star-shaped tiara twinkling in her hair; my father was resplendent in the uniform of a captain in the Scots Guards. His sense of humour was renowned and he soothed my nerves by telling me the last time he wore full dress uniform, before he had been wounded in the First World War. He was in the forecourt of Buckingham Palace drilling his platoon, prior to the Changing of the Guard, when to his horror he marched them straight into the railings because he couldn't remember the command to stop, let alone retreat.

The story made me giggle on the way to the Palace, the three of us in a huge Rolls-Royce which my mother thought the only appropriate form of transport and never mentioned that we had to hire it. I was still smiling, trying to do up the pearl buttons on my long white kid gloves which had to come over the elbow, when the car was stopped short by hundreds of people in The Mall waving at all the cars proceeding slowly to the vast gold and black gates. I thought it was awfully nice of them, considering we must have looked very theatrical and fancy-dressed.

On our arrival at the Sovereign's Entrance to the Palace I was parted from my parents and taken into a large ante-room where I found at least twenty other girls similarly attired, most of whom I knew. We just had time to exchange views about the hideousness of our dresses when a gentleman usher opened a door into what seemed like a throne room and told us to wait until our names were called and then to proceed individually.

I started to shake and feel sick but there was no going back now, no escape. I heard my name called, it was do or die, so with chin up, shoulders down, I began to walk forward. I had a blurred vision of a mass of people to my right. I think it was called an assembly and presumably my parents were among them. Twelve paces forward and there on the left were the Queen and the King. I curtseyed to the Queen first and did it without a wobble (thank you, Miss Vacani). I was just about to move on to His Majesty when a figure most regal caught my eye, sitting behind and between them. It was Queen Mary and I curtseyed to her before doing the same to the King. This, I was told afterwards with a gentle reprimand by another usher, was not correct but not a treasonable offence.

I think I did the middle curtsey out of instinct because Queen Mary was a friend of my grandmother and often came to tea with her at Eaton Place. I could never understand why my grandmother always put away her valuable collection of Russian snuffboxes and other china bijouterie whenever Queen Mary came to visit. When I asked her the reason for this concealment, she told me that if the Queen admired an object it meant she would like it as a gift and a refusal might mean the end of the friendship.

I thought she was quite beautiful, the epitome of a queen, dressed in Edwardian style with a high neck netted up to her chin, supported by tiny wires, and on top a small hat with a veil called a toque; but, for all her regal appearance, she had a sense of humour. When I was about four years old I was summoned to the drawing room from our nursery on the fourth floor to meet Queen Mary. Clutching on to Nanny, who had to wait outside the door, I was gently pushed into the presence. As I advanced towards this formidable lady my knickers fell down. I don't remember this embarrassing incident, but apparently I calmly stepped out of them as if nothing had happened. That's poise for you! Queen Mary laughed with pleasure and poor Nanny was mortified about having slipped up whilst sewing the elastic.

The rest of my upbringing was focused on education, languages and history taught to me by European governesses who were ignorant about the Plantagenets and Tudors. So I learnt about the French and Spanish instead. I didn't like the lessons, but then I didn't like the governesses either. When I returned from Germany at seventeen my mother decided I could educate myself and I became a bookworm, reading everything I could lay my hands on; but having reached the age of eighteen I was drawn by force down to London to be presented.

The rest of my debutante year remains largely out of focus and seemed to blend into one long dance. The really grand ones were called balls and on these occasions married ladies wore their tiaras, necklaces and bracelets and stomachers in sets of shimmering diamonds, rubies, emeralds and sapphires. Long white gloves were de rigueur at the beginning of the evening and then removed because it was considered vulgar to wear bracelets over them. Some of the jewels were so valuable that it was rumoured that some families had copies made to avoid the vast insurance premiums.

During the first year of "coming out" chaperoning was essential and considered correct. My poor mother escorted me to every dance preceded by a big dinner party. There she sat on a gold chair against the wall of the ballroom in some large townhouse until the early hours of the morning whilst I had the time of my life. Few fathers attended and the ones that did were pretty boring. She did get the odd offer of a dance because she was very beautiful. All my men friends sent her flowers and flirted with her.

On arrival at a dance you were given a small rectangular card which folded, with a small pencil attached by a silken cord. The card was numbered from one to twenty and the men had to ask you if you would dance with them. If you agreed they wrote their names on the appropriate number. This was an excellent formula, because if you took pity on a dullish chap who had pestered you all evening, you could always get rid of him for the next dance as the band stopped after each one.

I was lucky enough, due to my male childhood friends, never to be a wallflower. This unkind title was given to the not so pretty girls who didn't know any boys and after the obligatory dance with their dinner partners could not fill their cards and were forced to spend most of the evening sobbing in the ladies' cloakroom. It must have been a refined form of torture for them and not until the end of the season could they return to the bosom of their country estates and seek solace with their ponies and dogs.

And so I flitted happily from May to July, attending luncheons, cocktail parties, and the nights dancing at Holland House, Londonderry House, the Ritz and Claridge's, the latter two being the venue for those families who had no town residence. Then there were the important four days at Ascot races in June. I wore a different outfit each day and had to prominently display my Royal Enclosure badge; otherwise gentlemen in top hats and green velvet jackets would bar you entrance. Some people tried to get in without one but they never succeeded. Silk or tussore dresses should be worn with large straw hats to match and the inevitable white gloves, but this time they could be short. One poor girl was made to wear long dresses by her mother. That fashion had gone out two reigns before. I felt sorry for her, but wished she would wipe that vapid smile off her face.

My parents could not afford to give me a "Coming Out Ball", but my beloved godfather and his wife, Lord and Lady Louis Mountbatten, did so at Brook House in Park Lane and I shall never forget their generosity and the wonderful evening.

The question of ballgowns had presented a financial problem at the beginning of the season, which was tactfully solved by Victor Stiebel, a famous dress designer who offered to dress me for free. I had an eighteen and a half inch waist, which must have tempted him, and I had the choice of any gowns I wanted on condition that I gave them back at the end of the season or bought them for £20 each, which seemed reasonable enough, except that Victor Stiebel was intent on reducing my already tiny waist by fitting a sort of corset inside the dress called a guêpière. Unfortunately this resulted in my being unable to eat more than a crumb for dinner without feeling I was going to explode.

At the end of July nobody ("but nobody" as my grandmother used to say) would be seen dead in London and the whole of society moved north to Yorkshire and Scotland. I began the rounds of grouse shooting and stalking moorland stags from one stately home to another. A definite change of clothing was required, most of which I had already, but head covering was a must. An unfortunate fashion at that time was the beret, in any colour but red, of course, which would scare the birds. I looked perfectly hideous in one and would place it as far back on my head as possible, resulting in it flying off even in the merest breeze. I solved the problem by borrowing one of my grandfather's stalking caps with ear flaps that tied round your chin in a cold wind.

In every house I was invited to I always took notice of the furniture and pictures. I was lucky enough to be brought up in beautiful houses and had been taught to appreciate art in all forms. I would mention his fine possessions to my host, who was always pleased to hear a "young filly" extolling their virtues and I often secured a second glass of champagne as a result.

Most of these big houses had architectural additions to each side called wings. In one would be housed the servants. Others were known as bachelor wings where the unmarried men were placed. The girls, of course, were in the main part of the house to avoid what they called "hanky-panky" in the night hours. I did not know quite what this meant; it was also known as a bit of "ooh la la". I was soon enlightened and decided I did not want or dare to take part in such rompings.

September over, I was sent back to my grandmother's house in Scotland and, to my amazement, was only too happy to shed sophistication and enjoy a simple rural winter.

We were all back in London by October, by now missing the excitement of the earlier part of the year. I thought it would be a good idea to give a beer and sausage party. Our flat was big enough and it boasted a grand piano, which was strange as none of us could play it. I asked my mother's permission for this event. She gave it and suggested it always makes a good party if you mix up the generations.

She was quite right. It always makes more fun with different ages and especially as she was so pretty for her years. Of course the idea of beer and sausages went out of the window and something more sophisticated was placed on the menu. The number of guests grew by the minute; the older ones were thrilled that we were all nearly grown up and they no longer had to sit for hours on the gold chairs. My mother suggested that I found a pianist for the evening and took up the rugs in the hall for dancing.

I went out to dinner with my boyfriend of the moment a few evenings later. We dined and then decided to visit the Florida nightclub, newly decorated with a glass floor and coloured lights underneath. There was only a single man playing the piano and to our enormous delight he turned out to be Fats Waller, one of our favourite artistes. The place wasn't very full so we were able to talk to him. After a bit I mentioned my party and asked if he would come and play for us. I said it would be fine if he could visit my mother the next morning and discuss things. He seemed delighted to do so.

Having thought I had arranged the proceedings quite sensibly, it wasn't till he arrived at Grosvenor Square that I realised I had forgotten to tell my mother that he was an extremely large man. It took her a bit by surprise, but not for long. On reflection the ensuing conversation was very funny. She asked him how much he would charge for the evening. He replied, "Two thousand pounds with champagne and whisky chasers." "Out of the question," said my mother. She couldn't possibly afford it. Meantime, unknown to us, the theatrical grapevine had told him that several important guests were to be there, including Princess Marina of Kent. To my mother's astonishment, he said he would play for nothing. "Oh," she said, "that will not do. I would not contemplate such an idea. I will pay you twenty-five pounds for the evening plus champagne." She did not look too happy about the whisky and decided that one of her friends, Lord Sefton, would be deputised to take care of him and ensure that he kept reasonably sober. I don't think he had ever been given such an onerous task and had a frantic expression on his face all night. It was a wonderful evening with the grown-ups doing the foxtrot and us juniors using up all our energy dancing the Big Apple. We didn't think about a possible war and hoped that Hitler would go away.

THE PHONEY WAR

After this experience eighteen months went by full of fun and frolic and growing up, but behind it all was the uncertainty of European politics and the steady advance of Nazism both territorial and arbitrary. The German people seemed possessed by Adolf Hitler. Their adoration of him appeared fanatical and unbalanced. To the British he looked like a cartoon character, yet there was something deeply sinister behind that weird exterior. The Western world vacillated whilst he crept on, covering the carpet of Eastern Europe with his forces.

Perhaps we did not want to recognise the danger; also we were totally unprepared for war. There was enough pacifist talk at the time except for a few brave souls who spoke out, Winston Churchill amongst them. The young people of my generation fervently wished to stop the tide of emotional and physical fear which we felt was the result of pacifism, but people of my parents' and grandparents' age had already suffered the Boer War and the First World War with terrible casualties and loss of life. They were naturally repelled and mortally afraid of another destruction of their lives and loved ones.

In the early summer of 1939 my mother rented a small villa in the south of France at St. Maxime; it boasted a swimming pool, much to the delight of my brother and myself. It was an idyllic period amongst friends and family and we tried to forget the ominous clouds lurking beyond the French border.

On 25th August there was disturbing war news and my parents decided that a war was better spent at home. The next day we packed the minimum, all of us allowed one item; I chose a lipstick but my mother vetoed this and made me take a toothbrush instead, my brother buried our gramophone records under some mimosa shrubs, which I thought fairly unpromising, and at 2.30 p.m. we set off for the long drive to Paris.

Our car was an old Alvis which would have been roomy enough for us, but at the last minute a well-known Austrian film star turned up begging for a lift. He looked pale with terror and it seemed churlish to refuse him. It did make the journey extremely uncomfortable in the heat of the summer and we eventually reached the Ritz Hotel in Paris at 11.30 a.m. the next day looking very tired and crumpled.

There was no problem getting rooms, Paris seemed deserted. On the 27th my mother spent all day trying to get tickets on a boat back to England. Any boat would do. She queued all morning and finally succeeded. We left Paris for Calais immediately and dumped the car into the arms of a delighted fisherman.

It was a pretty foul voyage with the ship packed to the gunwales and a very heavy sea, so when the white cliffs of Dover came in sight like a beautiful dream I could have kissed the customs officer.

London seemed just the same, but I did not get much chance to verify this as my brother and I were packed off to Scotland to stay with our grandparents. On 1st September Hitler invaded Poland. This was the last straw in the desperate diplomatic tactics of the past year and on September 3rd Britain declared war on Germany.

Prime Minister Chamberlain's announcement of hostilities came over the wireless in my grandfather's library. Although expected, it was still a shock and through the trauma of digesting his sombre tones I heard my grandfather's parade ground voice ordering us to stand up for the National Anthem — he was a veteran of the Grenadier Guards. Hardly had those familiar strains faded when the air-raid sirens screamed out their mournful wail; my brother stood to attention like a toy soldier; my grandfather saluted, and I shivered. My grandmother, however, increased the volume on her hearing aid and suggested we should go up onto the roof with her binoculars. I wasn't too keen on the idea but fortunately the warning turned out to be a false alarm.

When invasion did not seem imminent, my brother was recalled to school and I stayed on in Scotland. My grandfather provided me with a fat but stalwart pony because I was to act as a despatch rider with messages from the house to the village some two miles away. I was armed with a .410 shotgun to repel any airborne raiders, the idea of bringing down a Heinkel bomber with a rabbit gun did not seem strange at the time, merely a sensible precaution.

Mobilization had by now taken place and I was rather isolated from other young people; but I discovered to my delight that the Royal Air Force had stationed a squadron of Hurricane fighters at an aerodrome just the other side of the woods which bordered the rather too large gardens of the house. The pilots were just as lonely as I was and only too pleased to be invited to dinner and have an evening away from the Mess.

It was a delightful situation, four or five glamorous fighter pilots all to myself to flirt with. They always sent their thanks for the hospitality by dropping a letter weighted by two pennies from a Hurricane on the front lawn. I don't know what the squadron commander would have said, but it prompted my grandmother's housekeeper to say, "It's a queer way to do your courting".

25

After three months of these rural defence duties I went back to London. The city had changed a lot, people seemed busier, with a sense of purpose. There was the blackout strictly enforced; doors had sandbags placed in front of them; barrage balloons filled the sky; weird-looking blimps floated on wires to prevent low-flying aircraft from attacking at close quarters. All the beautiful wrought-iron railings which had surrounded the London squares and parks had disappeared to be melted down for munitions.

My generation of males were all in uniform, a few of them wearing their regimental tunics with a modicum of vanity, and for a very short time we danced and played as if unaware of the oppression to come. I was out every night, unfettered, due to my age, by the attendance of a chaperone.

It was soon after all that veneer of joviality that my mother decided frivolity must come to an end and suggested that I get a full-time job. At that period of 1940 it was very difficult to get a serious war job, the Government had not had time to decide what girls could do. Cheering up the troops was simply not enough, so I was given forty-eight hours to find a suitable job and no messing about.

With much difficulty I found one on *Vogue* magazine, not aggressive enough but employment nevertheless and I occupied myself writing captions under the photographs of beautiful models. The aim was to persuade readers that fashion should have a military look. I thought it was tremendously patriotic and for this I was paid the princely sum of five shillings a week, which just about paid for my lunches and bus rides.

This job fortuitously did lead me into a short career as a freelance journalist and I wrote many pieces for the *Baltimore Sun*, a prestigious American newspaper. I managed to infiltrate the Holy Grail of all war correspondents, the Savoy Hotel. It was there that I wangled a meeting with Quentin Reynolds, a brilliant American journalist whose work and altruism towards the British was much admired. He told me over a drink in the bar that Hitler's father was an Austrian house painter and that his real name was Schicklgruber. That obscure piece of information made the journey home in the blackout almost agreeable.

It was an odd war when it started in September 1939. I was told wars always start after the harvest had been brought in, a wise move, I suppose, if you think it will only last a year. They called it the phoney war, because for a while nothing happened.

THE BATTLE OF BRITAIN

After the retreat from Dunkirk in May 1940 and the heroism of the men who sailed small boats across the Channel many times to rescue our troops, the French Army surrendered at Compiègne and most of France was occupied by the Germans, except for the south, where an undulating line ran from Bordeaux up to the Swiss frontier near Geneva. It was in that region that the now famous partisans called the Maquis were formed and many of our agents from S.O.E. were dropped by Lysander aircraft to join them.

In June 1940 Mussolini declared war on Great Britain. Nobody was too worried about that. The Italians had a reputation of disliking a fight and we thought it better to have them against us than on our side, a theory much underlined by some of our veteran servicemen who remained convinced that "abroad started at Dover".

We now stood alone against the mighty German Army and were determined to defend our island at all costs. Invasion was a strong possibility at this stage, which was a bit alarming. All the coastal areas were manned, concrete bunkers for guns built, and the church bells were silenced.

My career as a wartime journalist came to an abrupt end. I needed a more vital job and it was in August 1940, and the Battle of Britain, which was to be our baptism of fire.

My mother moved us to a small cottage in the country near Leatherhead in Surrey. It was conveniently close to London, but what she had not realised, poor darling, was that the location was slap bang in the middle of Bomb Alley, a stretch of country running from the south coast to the City of

London, which turned out to be the flight path of the German bombers after they had crossed the Channel. Every night, unless there was a blessed fog, their deep-throated engines could be heard thundering towards London and on the way back the pilots frequently jettisoned high-explosive bombs to lighten their loads and save fuel. The countryside was also the scene of many aerial dogfights, with Hurricanes and Spitfires battling it out against Messerschmitt 109 fighters who were protecting the Heinkel and Dornier bombers. These combats were terribly exciting to watch as they usually took place in the daytime and at low level, but it was so often heartbreaking to see some of our planes spiralling down in flames. Winston Churchill got it right in one of his famous speeches, when he said, "Never in the field of conflict was so much owed by so many to so few."

I often walked along the Downs, a long expanse of chalkland where you could see for miles. It was there one day that I witnessed the most spectacular dogfight. The planes were weaving about in tight circles, guns blazing and engines screaming. At one point a plane flew down towards me and, to my horror, I spotted the black swastika painted on the side of a Messerschmitt and the pilot had his guns aimed at me. Shaking with fright, I ran for the nearest clump of trees and threw myself into a pile of leaves like a frenzied mole, I could hear the bullets plopping all round me and I think that it was then I began to hate.

I did not tell my mother about this incident on my return to the cottage and fortunately she was busy stocking the cellar with canned Canadian maple syrup sent by a kind friend from overseas. She injected rat poison into several cans with a heavy syringe in case the Germans landed. I think she was convinced that I would be raped and was determined to kill off a few before the evil deed took place, but after a few weeks she could not remember which ones were lethal, so we were all denied that sweet indulgence.

We all did fairly pointless things at that time. I bred rabbits, dear little black and white creatures and very prolific. We ate them, which my brother thought was cruel, but they bred so rapidly that his suspicions were flummoxed by sheer weight of numbers and when cooked they were known as chicken; but he was soon to leave school and join the Grenadier Guards, so he forgot all about them.

My mother went to work in a munitions factory nearby which manufactured 4.2 naval guns and the work was exceptionally hard for one unused to manual labour. She came home exhausted in the evenings and was given supper by our maid, who had taken to the drink, carefully hiding the gin bottles under her bed.

I went to work as a telephonist at the local Air Raid Precautions Centre. It was my first taste of the dreaded night shift, I hated it because I could not sleep in the daytime, but the job was quite interesting. The air-raid wardens in the district would call in to report bomb damage from high explosives and landmines — the latter were the most destructive, devastating a large area. Our function after receiving the information was to alert the fire and ambulance services. They were stretched to the limit and due to the blackout they had to navigate without benefit of signposts, which had been taken down in the event of invasion. Not a chink of light showed through any curtains and the headlights of their vehicles were cut down to a mere slit.

One memorable night the army contacted us because they had captured a German pilot. He had parachuted down from his stricken bomber and did not appear to react to any questioning. This presented them with a language problem. Did we have anyone who could speak German? Fortunately, I happened to be on duty and was fetched by an army jeep. My imagination began to play strange tricks during the journey; my many months in Munich were to pay dividends, I was going to be able to spit in the face of the hated Nazi, curse the evil that made him, and stare at him with all the malevolence I could muster — this was payback time. Coming face to face with what I had supposed to be a subhuman hit me like rapidly awakening from a nightmare. There, crouched in the corner of an army drill hall, was an ashen-faced, shivering young boy — he could not have been much older than me. The shock stunned me into silence and I found that I could not hate him, but no way was I going to like him.

It took me two hours of cajolement and sensitivity to get his name and Luftwaffe number. It transpired that his silence and evident terror were due to the fact that he had been told that in the event of capture he would be tortured and then killed. I felt numb with disbelief at the repugnance of the Nazi propaganda machine and watched him being marched off to spend the rest of the war in a prisoner of war camp in some remote part of the British Isles.

I got a few petrol coupons for our small car, a sop for the draconian hours spent at the A.R.P. Report Centre. I went up to London whenever possible and dined with friends who were on leave. Some of them recovering from that epic feat, the evacuation of Dunkirk, which they preferred not to talk about, others were training for further conflict. You were not supposed to know this but one could tell by their stature, maturity and sometimes fleetingly sad expressions which mourned lost friends.

I still had friendly relationships with the American journalists and enjoyed their cheerful company. Of course there were a few cynical ones who thought we had already lost the war; you could not exactly blame them, things did look pretty bad, but it had a very irritating effect. I was asked out to dinner by one of these detractors. He was most attractive and despite his pessimistic views, I decided to accept, hoping that if I could not change his scepticism then at least I could give him a fright.

After a dinner of unparalleled excellence for wartime, I persuaded him to accompany me on a tour of the City of London. The area around St. Paul's Cathedral was taking its usual battering and was as noisy as ever, which gave him a terrifying initiation into the world of bombs and flames. The poor man was fairly shattered by this experience and thought a drink at the Dorchester Hotel in Park Lane would soothe his nerves. With the outstanding resilience of his nation he soon recovered and continued his soliloquy of how we would lose the war.

To underline his theme he pointed to the backs of seven R.A.F. pilots standing at the bar and asked me what on earth were they doing lounging around doing nothing. Biting back my anger, I went up to the bar and asked if they could turn round and face the gentleman over there. My journalist friend gasped and turned a shade pale, for in front of him were seven young men all with the Distinguished Flying Cross and Bar. He managed to splutter, "but they are all so young and just out of school"!

I do not know whether I did any good that evening but at least I had proved that we may be down but never out, and our spirits were unquenched.

THE BLITZ

Despite winning the Battle of Britain, the winter of 1940 brought fearful air raids on London and other major cities. As they began to increase, the monotonous drone of German bombers could be heard every night; the destruction and havoc sometimes brought very strange incidents, including a double-decker bus found balancing precariously three storeys up an apartment building, indicating the immense effect a bomb blast had on any person or object. Another night some poor woman was lifted by this power whilst in her bath and landed, still in the tub, in the street. She was covered in plaster, which had to be chipped by the firemen. The moral of that story is never be caught in an invidious position in an air raid. I usually favoured diving under the nearest table because, other than a direct hit, you were able to avoid being covered by bits of the ceiling falling down.

This Blitzkrieg was particularly hard for mothers with small children. Although worried and fatigued, they did jobs for the war effort as well as looking after their little ones. A majority of them had their anxiety relieved by the children being evacuated to the countryside. The poor little mites stood miserably in railway stations with large labels round their necks stating their name and destination. They were shepherded by kindly W.V.S. ladies who had more than enough to cope with, but on arrival they were welcomed with open arms by kindly country folk. A whole new world stretched in front of them. They were amazed and highly suspicious to find that milk came from a cow and not a bottle, and, in some cases, refused to drink it!

Those families left behind spent the darkened hours in Tube stations and shelters. The latter, in my opinion, were deathtraps, they stood on street corners built of brick and concrete about the size of a tennis court and had an awesome tendency to collapse, causing as much injury to the wretched people as the bombs.

In the Tube stations it was different, a true place of refuge and the families were often cheered by buskers who serenaded them. In the mornings they went home wondering if their houses were still standing, that was courage personified.

It is difficult to compare thoughts of today with those of the war years. As a younger generation, perhaps, we were scatterbrained and sometimes frightened, but we were resolute, with a fierce patriotic pride, determined to win; we had an adoration of anyone in the armed services and a cast-iron hatred of the enemy. Women hate easier than men because they do not have to do the killing.

At all times we were much invigorated by singing popular songs such as *Roll out the Barrel* and *Run Rabbit Run*, both pretty awful in retrospect but there was one particular favourite which went *Hitler has only got one ball, the other is in the Leeds Town Hall* sung to the tune of Colonel Bogey. Quite why his second testicle should be lodged in the civic centre of a town in Yorkshire I never did fathom, but it gave me enormous pleasure to sing it.

Like most of my friends I got used to going out in air raids. There was no point staying at home to be bombed. It was more tolerable to be out and about in the overhead danger; "why should those bastards get us down" seemed a reasonable enough philosophy.

On one particular evening whilst waiting for my boyfriend to pick me up, my thoughts were in a petulant state, I wondered if it would be another night of cacophony and would we ever get a respite from this continual battering? I had managed to be in nearly all the heavy London raids, more by bad luck than anything else; trust me to be given the night off in time for them. I put on what was left of my Chanel scent and dismissed apprehension.

The raid started as soon as we arrived at the Mirabelle restaurant in Curzon Street. Above the clamour of people's conversation came the noise of our trusty anti-aircraft guns in the distance, while more distinctly I could hear the sonorous hum of bombers overhead. The chatter continued on regardless, it did not help to be too silent, but it was going to be a noisy dinner. It always interested me that when you hear the thud of incendiaries the curtains never move; but when the crash is a high-explosive bomb the curtains blow inwards. I never did discover the scientific reason for such a movement and got on with eating my food.

When we left the restaurant there was an unnatural silence and I was certain there was more to come. The street was full of burning smells and fires blazed to act as beacons for the Luftwaffe. We took a brave taxi down Piccadilly and stopped to put out an incendiary bomb with a bucket of sand, not my favourite occupation in my only pair of high-heeled shoes; however, to my relief the voice of a fireman boomed in my ear, "Keep away, that's a gas main."

We ran back to the taxi, who had waited patiently for us, and drove on towards Leicester Square anxious to get to the 400 Club. That particular incendiary bomb in Piccadilly had inadvertently saved our lives, for we had by the closest of margins missed the devastating bomb which killed so many people at the Café de Paris situated just yards from the entrance to the Square. It was a popular place for dining and dancing because it was underground and thought to be safe. It was not until the rescue services had removed the pathetic mangled bodies that it was found to have a glass roof. Shattered we went on to the 400 Club.

After this bloodbath it might have seemed unworthy and shameful to continue the evening, but life has to go on. The 400 was packed with many people still shaken and shocked by the obliteration of the Café de Paris, we were all too troubled to express our feelings adequately even if there had been time to do so. More squadrons of German planes came over and I was dancing when the bombs came whistling down again. My prayers for bad weather had not been answered and so the battering of body and soul began once more.

We gave up dancing, it was like trying to balance on a board in a stormy ocean. Sitting was almost as difficult because the seats took to lifting themselves up in the air and crashing down again, fortunately landing in the same place. This bombardment went on for what seemed like an eternity; minutes dragged by and bombs flew down. I was terrified but luckily my terror was of the passive kind, I sat quite still unable to move, eat, drink or smoke. I only spoke when irritated by something such as when a young soldier suggested playing war games. I certainly lost my sense of humour during those four hours. I hoped it would return and the loss was due only to enforced inactivity.

The next instant we heard the detonation of a bomb very near. My heart thumped; I tried to stand but my legs wobbled. I sat down again and waited whilst the bottles and glasses fell off the tables and large rats emerged from behind the decorative red wall hangings. An air-raid warden staggered in and told us the high-explosive bomb had dropped next door

— the whole building was on fire and it was definitely time to leave.

Outside, the fire was enormous, my face felt scorched and my shoes turned from black to white. The heat from the ashes burnt through the soles and broken fragments of glass cut my ankles. The flames were an easy target for the Germans and the firemen told us to go away; there was nothing we could do to help.

I was not sure, not at all sure, but I thought the raid was over by then. There was a silence all of a sudden except for the crackling of the fires, the sky was dark blue, patchworked with smoky red exuding an acrid smell. Then came the all-clear sirens taken up like dozens of instruments in an orchestra and, as they died away, the roar of the burning buildings could be heard again. As London strove to breathe, the blessed dawn arrived to quench her fires, satisfy her thirst and bury her dead.

Getting about in the city was something of an assault course. The indomitable taxis were few and far between and you usually shared them with other people whilst dodging the bomb craters. I found it expedient to wear rough low-heeled shoes, presenting a comical sight with an evening dress, but it was easy enough to change into high heels in the ladies' cloakroom of a restaurant. The buses ran intermittently, which was hardly surprising, but run they did and when they turned up the drivers were carriers of mercy and understanding. On the route from Sloane Square to Piccadilly they would pull up opposite the Ritz Hotel, certainly not an official stop, but they never refused to do so and waved a cheery goodbye with the words "Have a good time, darling."

Being stuck in the A.R.P. Centre for days and nights on end was not my idea of spontaneous, unsolicited worthy work. To relieve the tedium and routine tied to a telephone, I usually spent the odd forty-eight hours' leave with a friend in London who was a member of the Women's Voluntary Service. She ran a mobile canteen for the fire services. These incredibly brave firemen endured hours dowsing flames and rescuing bomb victims together with the wardens.

I volunteered to go with her during one particularly rough night. We set off with supplies after dark; the sky was criss-crossed with searchlights like car windscreen wipers picking out the Heinkels and Dorniers for the anti-aircraft gunners. This particular mission of ours was unexceptional, a normal duty shift carrying tea urns, currant buns, biscuits and the much loved ubiquitous Woodbine cigarettes.

Our objective was the London Docks, which was taking its usual pounding, We needed no headlamps or guidance because flames pinpointed the area like a monstrous firework party. On arrival somewhere in Wapping, right on the River Thames, we encountered a wall of fire at least twenty foot high. This formed a barrier between two lots of firemen, and the ones nearest the river were cut off.

We had to make a quick decision. Those men needed food and drink and they were going to get it — the answer was simple but hot. If the firemen on our side played their water hoses on the canteen we could get through to them. The canteen, although a bit ancient, was a reliable old machine and in first gear she leapt through the flames like a superannuated greyhound. We appeared blistered but unharmed in triumph on the other side to the croaky cheers of blackened faces and cracked smiles. I felt a lump in my throat and tears in my eyes which was not entirely due to breathing smoke.

RATIONING

Travelling about became difficult due to the scarcity of fuel, but with my mother's petrol coupons given to her for her ordnance work and my few flimsies from the A.R.P. Centre we were not too housebound. We had enough to get to the railway station at Leatherhead only a few miles away and once there often waited hours for a train to arrive. There was something reassuring about a steam train with its puffing smoke and proud whistle. They stopped at every station on route and more frequently for air raids on the way up to London. The interiors were hardly salubrious due to lack of man- or woman-power to clean them, and we normally arrived at the terminus speckled with pieces of soot from the engine.

Food rationing was by then established, which made us all much healthier, although it did nothing for the tastebuds. We had ration books with coupons in them. For meat you had to register with a butcher and it was best to flirt with him, hoping for an ounce or two more. If you went away you took your book and gave it to the grateful hostess for the remainder of your stay.

On the ration book you were allowed 4 oz. of bacon or ham, 4 oz. of butter and 12 oz. of sugar each week. My butter never seemed to last the week and I was left with particularly nasty oily margarine. Later on even that was rationed to include 1 oz. of cheese to last seven days, hardly worth the purchase! There was a stressful scarcity of soap, so any remaining slivers of a tablet were carefully moulded together with the other bits to make a new bar. Chicken and fish were not rationed but trying to find any was a true test of ingenuity. You could buy whale meat, but the less said about that sustenance the better.

A lamb chop was a rare delicacy and soon any such protein was replaced by something in a tin called Spam sent over by our good friends — but not yet Allies — from across the Atlantic. When chopped up and cooked with reconstituted dried egg and embellished with young nettle tops, which tasted like spinach, the result made an astonishingly good omelette. Vegetables were very scarce and we had to queue for potatoes. This always surprised me because every patch of urban ground became an allotment. A married friend of mine kept chickens in her small London garden. She bought a cockerel to increase the flock much to the annoyance of her neighbours, who were awoken at an ungodly hour by his matutinal crowing and had to be placated by the odd egg.

The Black Market reared its ugly head, of course. Most of us thought it rotten and unpatriotic, although I have to admit I did not turn my nose up at a gift of half a dozen fresh eggs and didn't ask where they came from. Country people were the envy of townsfolk because they were allowed to keep a pig and eat it.

Clothing coupons were also introduced. It was a blow to the fashion-conscious. I used to swap my sweet ration with children and laboriously save them up to buy a dress. All new clothes, blankets, towels and linens were fabricated under the name of utility. We thought them dreadfully drab but fifty years later I still have use for the blankets. The question of make-up was very vexing. Although black boot polish made excellent mascara, you had to be careful not to laugh or cry, in which case you ended up with streaky blotches running down your face. Lipsticks were cherished and only applied for special occasions.

Our attempt at glamour to relieve the hardship of our existence was rather frustrated because by law we had to carry a gas mask. These were horrible things to wear and practically asphyxiated you, which should not have been the right effect. Fortunately we never had to use them. They came in black mock-leather cardboard box with a shoulder strap. It was the custom amongst the young and foolhardy such as myself to hide the mask under the bed, where it gathered dust. The container then became a receptacle for carrying purse, brush, make-up and the inevitable identity card with my number AYNR 11.2.

There were few compensations for the paucity of clothes, except that we were not required to appear in hat and gloves when visiting our elders and betters, but one great blow to the self-esteem was the lack of silk stockings. I tried woollen ones in the first winter months but they itched unbearably and so were discarded. Without short socks, which I thought childish, every shoe seemed to have a nail somewhere. I was tortured by chilblains, blisters and lack of sticking plasters to ease the sores and was at last resigned to the fact that we had no silk stockings. I did find a few laddered pairs at the back of my drawer which were quite useless until someone told me of a stocking renewal service at 200 Seven Sisters Road, London, N.4., but I never got there. It was surprising to see so many bright colours around but women felt if they could only buy one dress per year they wanted something brilliant, anything to enliven the murkiness of our lives. We did, however, have a lot of fun now and then remaking old clothes, converting evening dresses into underwear, men's trousers into skirts, and odd bits of wool into scarves. The poor men had little chance to remonstrate because they were mostly all in uniform. Summer sandals were hard to find, I tried to make a pair by cutting out old leather soles and bound them with coloured tape. The result was a complete disaster as they flapped with each step. Community clothes were a great help with friends lending out their dresses and the ancient system of barter was our sole non-coupon transformation.

Sometimes food parcels came from America; they were gifts to delight the stomach and soul. The best of them, although none was disregarded, contained butter and preserves. There were chocolate bars, lipsticks, and Kleenex tissues (much valued as loo paper — the stuff we had, often old newspapers, was deplorably rasping). Most prized of all were the nylon stockings. I manicured my toenails for hours for fear of snagging them and the silky feel of them was extraordinarily sensual.

In early 1942 the Yanks, as we called them, arrived on our shores. America had declared war on Japan and Germany as a result of the Japanese attack on the naval base at Pearl Harbor in the Hawaiian Islands. They did not want to fight a war any more than we did, I think distance had deceived them into the spirit of isolation, but this attack had jolted their false serenity and to our relief they joined us in the battle.

The immediate reaction of not having to fight alone is hard to describe. We had been a lonely little island since the fall of France and had to brace ourselves to strengthen our resolve, but now not counting the cost we would defeat Hitler and his evil periphery.

London was soon full of G.I.'s. They were green, unsophisticated youngsters who had most likely never stepped out of the United States before. We were very happy to see them but they did think they were God's gift to women and inclined to make passionate advances to almost any female who swam into their vision. The promise of nylon stockings often fulfilled their desires; but normally the astonished girl was rescued by the U.S. Military Police who proliferated the London streets and were known as Snowdrops because of their distinctive white helmets.

All American troops seemed much bemedalled and it was not long before we discovered that one particular gong called a Purple Heart was given for having been wounded even down to a scratch. This amazing piece of news caused a lot of hilarity and teasing which the G.I.'s took with their usual good humour.

FRIENDS

I had a great friend called Osla Benning, so named Osla because her mother thought the Norwegian city of Oslo most beautiful. Its namesake was just as lovely with dark hair, alabaster white skin, an exquisite figure and a gentle, loving nature to match this perfect combination.

She had been sent away to Canada soon after the war started and departed breathing resentment and fury. She spent the year of her exile plotting her return to England, much to the perplexity of the distant cousins who looked after her. They were baffled by the concept that anyone should want to return to a war-torn island. Her objective was finally achieved by flirting shamelessly with gentlemen of power and somehow managed to defraud someone out of an air ticket to Lisbon.

Having at last arrived in the Portuguese capital she found herself surrounded by spies cloaked as German diplomats. There were listening bugs behind every potted plant in the hotel in which she found accommodation. This dubious neutrality made it doubly difficult to pursue her scheme to get on a Catalina flying boat. Everyone listened to everybody. After months of frustration, money rapidly running out and frequent cables to us ending with adjectives such as 'desperate', 'miserable' and 'suicidal', she finally got a berth in a cargo ship bound for Liverpool.

The ship cavorted and zigzagged its way through the treacherous waters of the Bay of Biscay and the even more dangerous seas of Western Approaches between Ireland and England, dodging U-boats and their torpedoes which were dancing *Swan Lake* round the little ship's thin camouflaged skin. Osla slept on a straw mattress and consumed bread and watery soup for sustenance. A twenty-four-hour watch on the lookout for enemy shipping was imperative, hardly conducive to preparing gourmet meals and in no way could the gallant crew produce proper food.

After ten gruelling days and nights the ship docked in Liverpool. Osla returned to London by train, a triumphant but filthy waif who had to be bathed in carbolic and water by my mother and deloused by a reluctant hairdresser. I was deliriously happy to see her and so were her innumerable boyfriends.

On the subject of boyfriends I suppose I should mention sex, or the lack of it. I was just plain innocent without any feeling of awkwardness or embarrassment that purity might provide. The strange part was that although my brother and I had been brought up in a house with a home farm and had watched cattle coupling and chickens copulating as a routine affair called breeding, I simply did not associate it with human beings. I think we would have settled with delivery by winged fairies called Bluebell and Cowslip. I lived in a romantic cloud with dreams of falling in love and that was as far as it got.

Boyfriends were decent enough not to take advantage of this ingenuousness and saw to it that all girls of my disposition were returned safely to their hovering mothers after a night's revelling on the town. Having grown up a bit I finally understood that babies are neither found under gooseberry bushes nor delivered by elves.

We imagined that they would ease their frustrations by taking themselves off to a high-class brothel. There was one called the "Bag of Nails" run by a lady called Milly. No respectable girl was ever seen there. Speculation was rife amongst us as to actually what went on, but no amount of prodding would divulge the delights of such a spot.

During permissible social activities it was considered alright to hold hands, accept a chaste kiss and dance cheek to cheek, but the possibility of going any further was condemned because it was certain to lead to pregnancy and result in ostracism from one's community. To illustrate this preconceived notion, a pass made in a taxi was a danger signal and instantly rebuffed. Poor Osla was mortified one evening when she confided rather too loudly to a girl friend that her partner had misplaced his torch into his front trouser pocket. She got a withering look from an older woman opposite, who said, "You silly fool, don't you know what an erection is? It is time you went back to school and learnt elementary biology." The answer was she did not know but was not going to give the old trout the satisfaction of asking.

CALL UP AND RECRUITMENT

We had become an island fortress with Coastal Command, the Royal Air Force and the Home Guard to protect us, the latter have been known as Dad's Army but that affectionate nickname was not used until many years after the war. They were mostly too old or unfit to join any of the services and were veterans of the First World War, but one and all they were as tough and gallant as they come; prodigious characters with an inveterate sense of humour, they took the job very seriously. We had enormous confidence in them and felt sure they would save us from invasion.

In the spring of 1940 many young women had volunteered to do various jobs formerly undertaken by men for the war effort. Some went to work on the land, they did a hard day's work and sometimes spent the evenings in local pubs drinking beer or scrumpy. The customers were rather surprised and there was a bit of "oohing and aahing" but they had done a man's work and deserved a man's reward. Others went into factories filling the shells of guns with explosives; a good many joined the military services of which there were three, army, navy and air force; the girls did all kinds of jobs, some of them physically hard, like barrage balloon operators heaving the great blimps into the air. I was envious of the girls who flew completed aircraft from factory to airfield, but I was no pilot and had no chance to serve in that capacity. However, Osla and I decided it was time for serious action, we felt the jobs we were doing, although worthwhile, were not important enough because we were capable of more. Osla was fed up banging a typewriter at the War Office and I was not exactly stretched in mind and body at the A.R.P. Centre. After twenty-four hours of concentrated thought, we decided against joining any of the Women's Services. Leaving out the W.R.E.N.'s was a bit of a wrench because the uniform was so pretty.

We finally hit on the idea of manufacture. The most vital of all manufacturing was the need for aircraft, particularly fighter aircraft, as I had witnessed some of their destruction during the Battle of Britain and knew how much we needed them to protect us from enemy bombers. Ignoring the fact that I had absolutely no idea how to make an aeroplane and couldn't even change a tyre on a motor car, my only claim to mechanics was the ability to remove the rotor arm from a vehicle to prevent it being stolen by invasion troops. Our inspiration had spawned an intense desire to do something of the greatest priority. With this in mind we applied for an interview with the labour superintendent at the Hawker Siddeley factory at Colnbrook, near Slough in Berkshire which made Hurricane fighter planes. Much to my surprise we got the job and were told to report at 8 a.m. in two days' time. I fully expected to be turned down on grounds of incompatibility and lack of experience. They must have been pretty desperate to select us, but nevertheless I was thrilled to be part of the real war effort.

The state of euphoria at being accepted was slightly dampened by having to find accommodation nearby. Slough was an infinitely dreary place and not to be contemplated and we eventually found digs in a small hotel by the River Thames in Old Windsor which had the advantage of a bus stop outside. Our room was large, shabby but comfortable; it would be hard to heat but the low ceiling would help contain what little warmth we could achieve.

THE HAWKER HURRICANE FACTORY

Packing up, leaving London and the struggle to heave the wind-up gramophone plus a large box of records into the train (an encumbrance not to be denied) had left us tired and breathless; so after a meal of reasonable quality and impatient for the next day we fell asleep.

A few hours before dawn, darkness heralded the great day. It started with abundant exhilaration and ended with a sorrowful sense of stupidity and exasperation. With a mighty heave I threw myself out of bed at 6.30 a.m. wondering if I would be alive ten hours later. We took the bus in the inky cold darkness, apprehensive of being late, and arrived outside the gates of the factory. It was huge, even menacing, and gave one the impression of a small town with fortifications. To be confronted at any time by a converging mass of people is bewildering and I couldn't think what I was doing and had to put a brave show of determination and hope no one would notice my knees knocking together.

We went straight to the labour superintendent as instructed. We had been interviewed by him previously and thought him a pleasant enough man. I signed a mass of forms which I was given no opportunity to read, except for one agreeing to pay one penny per week out of my meagre wages as funeral tax, not a happy thought to start the day. Business matters completed and Osla to follow shortly, I followed him to the medical department and was handed over to Matron-in-Charge. What a sight! Her uniform was starched up to her chin and she glared at me as she told me to undress for an examination. The thin gown she threw at me did not keep out the cold nor did it stop my shivers. At that point a lot of health talks ensued, all meant to be highly instructive, but I could have done with a medical dictionary. I felt distinctly unwashed and was dismissed by this Medusa.

Later, under guidance, I proceeded for what seemed an immense distance due south-west, I cannot think what possessed me to consider compass points. The trek ended in the training school where Osla and I were to learn to be aircraft mechanical fitters.

In an aircraft factory each department has a name which clearly tells you what it does. To my hazy recollection, on the way to the school, we passed through the crash shop, which had nothing to do with crashes; the wing shop; the dope shop; the paint shop and from there into the erection shop. There's that word again! The whole process begins with skeleton frames and ends up way over the other side with the finished Hurricane. The next step was to wheel them out onto the flying field, where a proficient pilot tests the completed product. I doubted if I would ever get to the dizzy heights of the erection shop, let alone watch a plane I had helped manufacture fly; but one can dream. Meanwhile, this whole unexplored territory and panorama was exciting and accentuated by the roar of planes overhead.

The training school was a fairly small section of this vast factory, unenclosed with no more than fifteen girls working on waist-high benches. Osla had by now caught up with me, equally startled by the funeral tax and muttering about a pauper's grave. Our guide introduced us to our tutor and departed. I was surprised by the clothes the girls wore. I had managed to procure a boiler suit which I thought suitable, but all the other trainees were dressed in fancy outfits adorned with plenty of make-up and an abundance of jewellery, bracelets and brooches that shone like icicles on their multi-coloured sweaters. It was not until later that I discovered they had no option but to wear their own clothes. Protective clothing was not provided by the management, pay was relatively low during training but fortunately cleaner work than on the production line itself. Dyed blondes and redheads were much in evidence; the combination of henna heads and coloured bodies made them look like a congregation of privileged peacocks, but they were friendly and gregarious and just as translocated as we were.

I don't remember learning anything much that first day. We were just thankful to catch the bus home to the sanctuary of our hotel room, ease the aching feet, eat a quick meal and collapse into bed. The next day our tutor taught me how to drill metal. I was hopeless at it and kept breaking the needle-fine steel drills one after another. I felt tears of frustration welling up in my eyes but it is a knack and once you get it life becomes bearable again. The metal I drilled was called Dural; it was an alloy of which planes were made. I tried hard to do the job without breakages, I even drilled in my sleep until I mastered the process, but my triumph was short-lived. There were further problems to overcome, namely riveting, filing, counter-sinking and pot-riveting, all equally daunting tasks for a beginner, but I got to quite fancy myself as a riveter and even got a commendation from the chief instructor.

Time became a very interesting factor and very important. I would steel myself not to look too many times at the large clock on the wall which ticked so slowly whilst hunger pains afflicted my stomach. Breakfast had seemed light years ago and then after what seemed an eternity, at the magic hour of 10 a.m., we had a fifteen-minute break. The bell rang and the sound of it prompted a stampede for the tea trolley. I ran like everybody else but often wondered why, the tea came out of a huge urn and tasted like bicarbonate of soda and the buns could crack the strongest of molars.

The lunch hour was from 12.30 to 1.30 p.m. We, being the whole factory, trooped off to the canteen herded together like so many sheep, the only difference being that sheep huddle together and don't have to queue in long parallel lines. We used to have concerts whilst we ate, "workers of the world unite" type of music with the occasional Glenn Miller swing band to cheer us up. These melodies blared forth from tannoys at each corner of the room's proportions, assaulting the eardrums. There was another break at 4 p.m. with more of the uneatable and undrinkable, but it gave us a chance to grumble about our aching backs and chafed feet. We worked on until 6 p.m. after which Osla and I staggered back to our "digs" almost prostrate with fatigue. Curiously enough the arrival, at about eight o'clock on some evenings, of friends in the Life Guards stationed at Windsor seemed to instantly revive our flagging spirits and weariness was temporarily forgotten.

When Osla and I had been in the factory for two weeks we decided to join the Transport and General Workers Union. Membership subscription was only a few pennies a week. My interest at first was purely academic and I was frankly curious, but I soon discovered how helpful it could be. Our shop steward, called Ted, was excellent at his job and ready at all times to listen to one's troubles, however trivial they seemed. He would go to the management on behalf of one of his members who complained about a draught down the back of his neck. This might be termed petty but an onslaught of cold air from behind for ten hours could cause a man to go sick and hold up production. He was equally brilliant with grumblers and moaners and managed to give them some degree of comfort without letting them slack off. In the language of trade unions at that period there was a popular saying — "I have my rights". I never quite gathered when one was supposed to express it and to what extent it applied, but it had a certain optimistic ring about it.

The duration of my training would take about three months, after which I would become a qualified semi-skilled mechanic. There is a contradiction in terms there, but that was my entitlement and I was going to earn it and proudly keep it. Along the line I learnt a lifetime of elementary mechanical engineering, or so I thought, until one day I was confronted with a blueprint of some mysterious part of an airplane. I was horrified, being no mathematician, and almost blinded at the sight of numerals I went all wobbly, but my instructor, a man of twelve years' technical experience, explained it to me in five minutes. From that moment on I was able to rattle off decimal points, use a slide rule with no difficulty, and would have gladly made the whole Hurricane if asked.

Those few months in the factory taught me many things. I learnt to keep my mouth shut about my family and personal life in the somewhat alien surroundings. I enjoyed listening to other people's stories about their relations, friends and lovers. I made friends with most of the girls, but some of them were nice to your face and turned on you behind your back. I came to the conclusion it was the survival of the fittest and I also discovered that whatever the characters, good or bad, the further production of aircraft, tanks and guns was their priority and vision to win the war.

The political and strategic spectrum had melded together in the belief that a concentrated effort by the workforce could succeed in this strife. It brought all the body politic and ideology together from the darkest blue Tories to the red-hot

Communists. The occasional Marxist voice was treated with the contempt it rightly deserved. Overtime became compulsory by the workers themselves; stories of absenteeism were grossly exaggerated and anyway, it was impossible to sneak a day off without a doctor's certificate. The rare break was sometimes necessary, you couldn't win a war through exhaustion and the hours we put in were certainly conducive to physical and mental stress.

PENNY ROYAL COTTAGE

After some weeks of desolate bus rides and a bleak hotel room, Osla and I got a huge bonus. My father had recently bought a small cottage in a village called Hedgerley, near Farnham Common, which was only a few miles from the factory site. Although my parents were separated, they always remained close friends and both were happy with the arrangement that Osla and I should live with him, so with great joy we moved into the comfort of Penny Royal.

My father had been badly wounded in the 1914-1918 war which had left him with a broken back, and he regarded looking after us as his war work, along with his job as a director of Pinewood Studios, where many wonderful movies were made. He would get up at 5.30 a.m. to light the fire and cook us porridge for breakfast. It was a bit stodgy at first but for a man who had never boiled an egg, it was a triumph.

Another bit of luck was the continued presence of the army at Victoria Barracks, Windsor, only five miles away. A lot of our friends were based there before being sent abroad and we had the pleasure and company of boys our own age most evenings. Penny Royal became the focus of entertainment for them and other friends from London who had to sleep on the floor, for the cottage was very small. The food was a bit dicey and sparse of choice; quantity rather than quality was the order of the day, potatoes being the mainstay. My indulgent father would sit beaming, pretending to enjoy the endless jazz music on the gramophone.

Every eighth day I had twenty-four hours off. Each moment was precious, so much so that the minute I left the factory gate, night bag in hand, I stood on the main Slough to London road and hitched a lift to the city. The transport that did stop for me was hardly salubrious, but what did I care, I was dressed for the part, steel filings and all. I usually stayed at Claridge's Hotel in Mayfair, which cost three pounds a night with breakfast, a lot of money in these days but worth it even on my small pay packet. Mr. Gibbs, the famous hall porter, was a patriarchal figure and much respected. He became our social secretary, which I think he rather enjoyed since he had known most of us since childhood, the days of tea parties, nannies and white gloves. On arrival he would tell us who was in town, hand out messages and suggest suitable venues as to where we should all foregather. This kindness was of invaluable help because telephonic communications were usually disrupted by bombs. I think he was an old matchmaker at heart and he often turned a blind eye when I deposited myself clad in the filthy boiler suit on the immaculate chairs of the elegantly furnished main lounge. I did it to torment and hopefully intrigue those who had never seen a factory assembly worker in such magnificent surroundings; it was done in the spirit of fun but I soon realised it was patronising and am ashamed of the recollection.

Slowly the weeks and months went by and Osla and I qualified to graduate from the training school. Of course, I had grandiose ideas of marching straight into the erection shop waving my qualifications, I had dreams of flirting with the test pilots whilst casually checking the almost complete Hurricane. No such luck! I was dispatched to a section which wired the cannon gun onto the Typhoons. This was a new type of aircraft, heavier than the Hurricane, highly armed and manoeuvrable. The Hurricane, although not as fast as the Spitfire, had a thicker skin and was capable of taking a lot of flak and punishment. They carried eight guns in the wings but these guns were immobile, forcing the pilot to face the plane towards the enemy. No wonder they were flung about all over the place and it was a miracle they stayed in one piece. Working on the Typhoon was an immensely complicated job and fearsome because of the anxiety that crossed wires could lead to a right ticking off from the foreman, and one could be immediately downgraded.

To solve the chilly problem of waiting for buses at dawn and at the end of a long day, Osla decided to buy a second-hand car. We found an ancient Alvis whose equally ancient owner was forced to part with it. My father approved of the make but not the age and was doubtful about the mileage, but the deal was concluded and she was the proud owner of her first automobile. I wanted to call it Hesperus because its appearance was a bit of a wreck but Osla decided it sounded too pessimistic and christened it Victor. With our petrol allowance of four gallons a month, which prohibited joy riding, we were able to cruise to work. This produced excellent results in fine weather but the following winter brought forth problems; Victor, on cold and icy mornings, refused to go up hill. Admittedly the village one was a bit steep and the only way to get round this difficulty was to retreat all the way back to the flat bit of road, press the accelerator right down and pray. The old heap was an alcoholic when it came to guzzling petrol and we only just lasted the month on our ration.

Sometimes we attended trade union meetings in the evenings at a pub near the factory. Victor could manage this as it was downhill all the way home and if you coasted in neutral it saved a lot of precious fuel. The subject matter of these meetings was allegedly "Further Production"; nothing was farther from the truth as far as I could make out. The assembly was tuned to drinking large quantities of ersatz beer and glorifying the Party. "What party?" I asked myself, because no one took any political stand very seriously, except to refer to those present as Brother and Sister. Osla and I came to the conclusion it was all a total waste of time and never attended again.

It was three months later that the blow struck. Disaster came in the shape of a directive to us two semi-skilled mechanics. Personnel was urgently needed in a small parts factory on the Slough Trading Estate. The transfer was immediate, with no hope of negotiation or preference. It was the Council of Despair, for Osla and I had been taught to make beautiful airplanes not bits of things; so in a truculent and rebellious mood we promised to report for duty the next day.

THE SLOUGH TRADING ESTATE

The spare parts factory was a dirty-grey square building sited amongst other dirty-grey concrete buildings. A truly bleak prospect which only increased our foreboding of what was to come.

During our first interview with the manager we diagnosed him as an obnoxious bully with an oversized inferiority complex and in return it was patently obvious that his diagnosis had designated us as a couple of prostitutes with strange accents. I reckoned that he thought he was inferior but wanted to be superior and the result was an extreme personality disorder. How true that proved to be. He dismissed our newly found skills as futile and time-wasting, which caused a leaden mantle of depression to descend upon our already overburdened souls.

Without any explanation as to the work we were supposed to do, he ordered us to proceed straight to Sister in the medical room. She came in the shape of a monstrous gargoyle belching dislike and hostility. The lady at Colnbrook seemed charitable in comparison with this harridan. The lecture began as soon as I sat down. It was not in the form of a consultation, more the staccato firing of questions, most of which were insulting and went as follows: Had I been treated for venereal disease? How many men did I consort with? How many times a week did I have a bath?

I knew by then that this pathological third degree had something to do with my way of speaking and the abrupt answers I gave her. I clearly had the wrong accent, which made me appear out of place and foreign to her, presenting some kind of threat. It was clear that nothing could be done to soften the insensitivity of this woman, so I just sat there trying to look hard and uncaring. It must be immensely frustrating to a prosecutor probing to catch you out if you exhibit dumb insolence. Osla fared no better but was brave enough to express her umbrage verbally.

On our return from this bloodthirsty grilling in the medical room, we were ordered to report to a part of the factory which appeared at first glance to have a black and dusty atmosphere, making it hard to see what was going on. Then, to my horror, I realised that women with dirty faces were occupied by drilling, the dreaded drilling. Sheets of metal Dural taking up most of the allotted space of the work benches were being drilled with hundreds of holes along each side in preparation for rivets.

This was to be my job for many months to come and the tedium was only relieved by news on the war front, some of it good and some of it bad. There was a new terror for British cities, German bombers renewed their attacks by dropping incendiaries followed by landmines which descended by parachute and exploded on impact, causing obliterative damage to any street or building. The attacks were so fearsome it was a miracle the spirit of the people survived. In early May five hundred bombers inflicted such destruction that next morning black smoke concealed the sun. Meanwhile, Hitler seemed to have lost interest in invading us and turned his evil tentacles towards Russia. He must have forgotten what happened to Napoleon... America was doing her best to clear the Atlantic of U-boats, but was not particularly successful in this objective.

However, there were good tidings which made us jump for joy. A bulletin issued by the BBC informed the British public that the great pocket battleship *Bismarck* had been sunk off the north-west coast of France. She had been a terrible threat to our shipping, having already sunk H.M.S. *Hood* as well as putting H.M.S. *Prince of Wales* out of action. Her last moments began the day before when a Swordfish from the aircraft carrier *Ark Royal* scored a hit with a torpedo as *Bismarck* was making for the ports of Brest or St. Nazaire. It crippled her rudder and propellers, forcing her to steam helplessly in circles like a wounded whale and allowed her to be battered by the *King George V* and *Rodney*, although these big ships were running short of fuel and Admiralty ordered them home. It was left to H.M.S. *Dorsetshire* to finish her off with torpedoes but *Bismarck's* Captain, Admiral Lutjens, had other ideas. He had already given orders to scuttle her.

Back in the factory I don't suppose anyone broke as many drills as I did. They were not all that fine but unless they went in dead straight they snapped. The man in charge of the stores department became a friend because I had to request replacements so often. I think even his patience was a bit strained until I got the knack of standing on tiptoes to whirl them in.

The canteen food was repellent and competed with the rest of the factory in an attempt to undermine all effort and sanity. The atmosphere of the workbenches was choking. My eyes, nostrils and mouth after an eight-hour shift were full of scratching metal dust and even the regulatory three-inch bath did little to relieve the irritation.

However, even purgatory had its rewards. The women and girls we worked with were angels from all walks of life, they were kind and reassuring with an indomitable sense of humour that no mean management could suppress. Osla and I loved them all, especially their fortitude and impudence. Our immediate best friends who worked on the same bench were four lovely ladies called Gert, Flo, Doris and Daisy. Stalwart they came and resolute they stayed. Although we were all uniformly dressed in dirty boiler suits, the girls spotted a difference. I think it must have been our funny voices. We had not yet learnt the correct four letter words and when to use them, but that did not seem to prevent compatibility.

The conversations ranged over the hubbub of drills on many topics. Gert, who had a permanent wave once every three months (self-applied, I think), kept a hairnet on from one application to another. She loved little waves and it was hard to tell where one stopped and the other started. She liked to talk about the good old days when she sold suspenders and other uplifting garments in Selfridges in Oxford Street. It was a highly respectable job she told me and I was very impressed.

Daisy waxed lyrical about her love life and the intoxicating encounters with her boyfriend, Bill. He had a bad leg which kept him from taking part in active service. Gout was suspected due to his proclivity to alcohol and tactfully never mentioned. He was therefore much in demand as an air-raid warden, as well as a permanent escort for Daisy. I thought her stories of seduction most romantic until she showed me a photograph of the famous fiancé. Frankly, I was dumbstruck at his countenance, which was most unprepossessing. I managed to stammer out that he looked as if he had a great sense of humour. Luckily this delighted Daisy, who thought him an Adonis, and the remark merely served to underline his already fine qualities.

Flo was married to an army sergeant serving overseas, she didn't know where but got letters posted via the military airgraph service. These were pieces of paper measuring four by five inches and appeared to have been photographed, space for any text was minuscule; just as well, perhaps, for they were not allowed, due to censorship, to write anything about army movements. Doris lived at home in Slough looking after her crotchety invalid mother. The factory was the full extent of her social life and she was one of the few who looked forward to the daily grind.

Everybody talked about their jobs before the war but Osla and I knew that despite our absorbing interest in the lives of others, the question of what we had done before 1939 was bound to crop up sooner or later. The Sword of Damocles hung over us with its single thread; we could not admit to the shame of never having had a job, I felt the knowledge might ruin our precious newfound friendships and make us outcasts.

When the time finally came, it was Gert who asked the question. I flustered and pretended to break a drill, Osla blushed to the roots of her hair, and in desperation we asked them to guess our previous occupations, hoping to put off the evil moment. "I know," shouted Doris above the din. "You were mannequins at Selfridges." Gert snorted and said, "Don't be daft, I'd 'ave heard about it in corsets and suspenders."

There was continued conjecture about our pre-war vocation, all of it getting more absurd and fanciful by the minute, when Osla, never short of a brainwave, said, "To tell you the truth we were fan dancers." Whilst this amazing revelation was being digested and our mortification hopefully evident due to such a sinful occupation, these loyal friends prepared themselves with their usual benevolence to ask for further information. "How many fans do you use?" asked Daisy, now rather worried by her invitation to meet her Bill in the pub one night and the thought of introducing him to two such notorious females. Osla replied with her quick intellect, "Three of course." When the question came to me, I lost my head completely and said "Two". You could feel the hush over the noise of the machines and I wished the floor would swallow me up.

However, to my intense relief, instead of the relevant enquiries as to which portion of my anatomy the two fans were placed, the hush was replaced by peals of laughter at such an outrageous fib and for the rest of the day I was the heroine of the section.

It was not long after this hilarity that the guessing game had to end, you could not spend eight hours a day, seven days a week with such philanthropic people and live the life of a lie. Judgement day had arrived. Flanked by Gert, Flo, Daisy and Doris in the canteen over a plate of repulsive baked beans we spilled out the awful truth, praying for forgiveness and atonement. We had done absolutely nothing before the war except dance and play around London as debutantes, wearing long frocks every evening and what was worse, my father was a Lord and my mother a Lady, the latter's status hopefully mitigated by the fact that she also worked in a factory.

Waiting for the axe to fall was painful but the anguish did not last long. Gert, the declared spokeswoman, said she didn't exactly know what a debutante was, but under the circumstances she felt it had been the correct thing to do. She did, however, want more than anything to meet a Lord and could they all come to tea the following Sunday? My patient father fell in with the idea with his usual tolerance but with some concern in case they should expect him to appear in his peer's robes. The tea party was a great success, although my culinary efforts at making scones was a disaster, but we all had fun together with many jokes and witticisms being exchanged. Gert's sartorial splendour for the occasion could only rival that of a Pearly Queen from London's East End. Where she didn't have buttons she had bows. Daisy took a great fancy to my father and instantly christened him "Lordie". She wagged a finger at him and said, if it was the last thing on earth she did, she was going to make Bill jealous. At this point we implored her to give up the idea because Bill had the reputation of being a practised pugilist and after several pints of beer could knock out almost anyone, bad leg notwithstanding.

FIGHT FOR THE FACTORY
WORKFORCE

The appalling conditions in the factory were getting us all down, but now we were somewhat cheered by writing and receiving letters to and from friends who had been taken as prisoners of war. I cannot remember exactly how we addressed the envelopes, it must have been through the International Red Cross, but I desperately hoped that they were received and wrote as cheerfully as I could with snippets of news that would not offend the Germans. Our prisoners, when not planning to escape, became very clever at disguising their words to confuse the stringent German censorship. A classic example was to pen a letter full of praise as to their welfare and end with the words, "Tell it to the army, tell it to the navy and tell it to the marines." It was a tried-and-tested phrase from many generations meaning, "Don't believe a word of it, it's all a bloody lie."

I heard about a brilliant cryptic remark written by a very chubby friend in a letter home to his uncle, who was a well-known racehorse trainer. In this letter he wrote the usual rubbish about the decent diet they were getting but adding that on his return he would be able to exercise the two-year-olds. This last piece of information was all his worried uncle needed to know. He must have lost a lot of weight due to lack of proper food because only lightweights could ride two-year-old horses.

In the factory time passed slowly and periods of exhaustion set in for both of us. I had to take the odd day off and lie in bed fighting constant fatigue. I became very anaemic and the same disorder afflicted Osla. It was a fairly shattering diagnosis, but we were determined to carry on because we had decided to try and right the wrongs taking place in the factory. There was so much to put right: the airless workplace, the indescribable food, the damp floors which even soaked through the wooden clogs we wore on our feet, the twit of the shop steward who hadn't the courage of a flea, but worst of all was the bullying and oppressive attitude of the manager. With the inspiration handed down to us by the Suffragettes earlier in the century, Osla and I decided the only answer lay in going to the top and that was at the Ministry of Labour in London.

We made an appointment with somebody in some department and spent hours drafting an appeal with very little hope of getting a genuine hearing, let alone a decision. In fact, we were rather frightened of being thought insolent, dismissed as ignoramuses and getting a black mark against our record; but it was too late to change our minds and off we went like lambs to the slaughter. The day before our trip up to London, the drilling section, who were naturally privy to our attack on the corridors of power, could hardly contain themselves with anxiety but they had to keep the mission secret at all costs. Doris lent me her silver horseshoe charm. Osla was armed with a piece of tattered white heather bought from a gypsy many moons ago. Gert shed a few tears and thought she would never see us again. I think imprisonment was looming in the forefront of her mind.

Wearing rather grimy boiler suits to create the right impression, we landed on the imposing doorsteps of the Ministry in St James's Square carrying our list of complaints, carefully edited to exclude any trivialities. We stood there externally proud in appearance but petrified under the skin, and Osla muttered something about bravery in action as the huge doors swung open to admit us. We were shown into an office with a big desk, behind which sat a man with the nicest and most amiable of expressions — it was many years after the war that I learnt he was the son of the famous crime writer, Edgar Wallace. He listened attentively to our story of woe, seemed to understand our altruism and that we were fighting for every soul in the factory. He thanked us for coming and twenty minutes later we were out again on our way back to Slough.

On the way back to Paddington station I felt sick by the thought that we might have failed and on arrival our spirits had to be bolstered by a sneaky beer in the bar. Once on the train I felt quite drunk and I was sure the unaccustomed liquor had gone to Osla's head because she made several speeches to sundry fellow passengers about the female of the species being deadlier than the male.

Amazing though it proved to be, our expedition to the Ministry succeeded beyond anyone's wildest dreams. Two weeks later the egregious manager just disappeared as if in a puff of smoke, to be replaced by a fair and sincere man. The whole aura of bleakness changed as if by magic; many less drills were broken; laughter took the place of tears; Daisy persuaded Bill to set a wedding date and Gert celebrated with a new perm, casting aside the ubiquitous hairnet.

RECRUITMENT TO A NEW JOB

Unknown to us, our life at the factory was drawing to a close, because two days later I received an official brown envelope stamped H.M.S. requesting me to attend a labour exchange in Sardinia Street near Lincoln's Inn. I think the word "request" was a polite way of saying, "Be there or else." Thank heavens, Osla got one too. It was patently clear we were to be removed from the factory; but where to and what for God only knew. I just hoped I would be able to contribute something more to Britain's war effort than drilling holes in bits of metal. Human frailty being what it is, I was physically drained but emotionally distressed at having to say goodbye to our faithful friends who had sustained us through the months of sweat and toil. A tearful farewell took place. We swore eternal friendship without actually drawing blood and promised to keep in touch. The relief of being able to abandon the slum-like environment of the Slough Trading Estate transcended the feeling of defeat and gave us a sense of elation.

Of course we had to leave the comfort of Penny Royal. I think my father missed us and I felt rather bereaved without him. It had always been a solace to come home and find a paternal interest in the happenings of our day; fortunately, he was starting on a war film and was pretty busy. I don't suppose he missed making porridge at 6 a.m. every morning. Of course we had to move up to London, leaving Victor behind. I don't think his engine would have managed the journey. I borrowed a small apartment in Victoria from a friend, who had gone overseas, as temporary accommodation and there we sat wondering what to do next. London was cold because coal was now rationed. At Penny Royal we had kept warm by gathering sticks and logs from the nearby woods, but here, to make matters more difficult, potatoes were hard to find and we didn't seem to find any friends in London.

The pragmatic official brown envelope had told us to report to Sardinia Street as soon as possible. Fortunately for us, a senior army officer and distant relative of Osla's advised us by telephone that they were searching for linguists and that we should be discreet about the visit because Special Intelligence was recruiting for German-speaking staff. A few years had gone by since I had been bilingual in that language and I was naturally apprehensive as to whether I would be accepted.

The appointment was made and Osla and I duly reported for what turned out to be a test of proficiency in the language. A grey-haired, stern-looking lady interviewed me and I seemed to pass her exacting oral and written exam. I was so relieved about this that I had the effrontery to ask her if she wished to hear my other linguistic achievements. It was an awful risk and I cannot think what possessed me to blurt this out. French would be easy. All those childhood years with Gallic governesses would pay dividends, holidays in France well remembered and happy hours reading Balzac, Verlaine and the daring sexual stories by Baudelaire. Any other language would be a nightmare but I was in the deep end and no way out.

My inquisitor did not appear very interested; in fact, her eyes became slightly glazed with frequent glances at her wristwatch, hoping I would not step beyond the bounds of credibility. Her manner prompted me to ask if I could express my fluency in French, Spanish and Portuguese. Before she could reply I launched into quotes of Proust, along with a bit of Victor Hugo, and she managed a watery smile. I could speak neither of the last two languages and instinct told me nor could she, so with all the courage I could muster I spoke the only words I knew in Spanish, which were *"Hasta la vista"* and *"Ole Toro."* If those words are pronounced very quickly they sound reasonable enough. In Portuguese I remembered the words for scrambled eggs and dragged the consonants out. The poor lady was by now bored to tears, desperate to get on with her next appointment and only too glad to get rid of me. She thereby, with unseemly haste, classified me as a multiple linguist. Osla found the German test easy and with her usual charm ignored the Hispanics and volunteered a stream of Greek verbs which she had learned in her spare time. The result was the same, a multilinguist.

I had no idea at the time what this test was all about nor what it would lead to, but it was clear that if I was going to be employed by this X factor, at least I was going to be able to use my brain. My thought processes had been rusticating for so long I could only pray for the probity of their return. We sat in the gloomy Victoria flat with nothing to do and afraid to go away in case a summons arrived. About two weeks later a letter came in the post bearing the initials H.M.G. For one awful moment I thought it might be a tax demand accruing from my miserable factory salary and I opened it with some agitation. The statement inside was bald and read: "You are to report to Station X at Bletchley Park, Buckinghamshire in four days' time." The second paragraph was equally terse, it merely said,

Your postal address is Box 111, c/o The Foreign Office. That is all you need to know.

Signed
Commander Travis

Osla had received the same communication, for which I was truly thankful. The thought of going unaccompanied to an unknown place, ignorant of what I was supposed to do, alarmed me. My parents accepted that my strange disappearance was inevitable and were quite philosophical about it. My mother's eyes had a gleam of envy in them, but then she had always been more adventurous than me.

I spent the next three days packing and unpacking — what on earth do you take for a wardrobe when you have no idea what the job is? For all I knew I might be going down a coal mine or servicing bombers on a cold airfield, but logic came to my rescue; neither of those occupations demanded the German language. I ended up filling the battered brown cardboard suitcase with the bare essentials of clothing, a toothbrush, half a tube of toothpaste, my teddy bear, the cosmetic warpaint and of course the wind-up gramophone.

THE INTRODUCTION TO STATION X

It was early Spring in 1941 that Osla and I took the train from Euston terminus to Bletchley, about forty miles north of London. It lay between Oxford and Cambridge, which I later came to learn was of considerable importance. The journey was not without incident and one that I should not wish to repeat. I was gazing out of the window admiring the farmland, which after the ugliness of industrial scenery looked very beautiful, when Osla started to nudge me in the ribs. I tried to ignore her without success, but she hissed at me in a stage whisper.

"That man across the compartment is doing something very peculiar." Indeed he was and to a part of his body to which I shall not refer. Pink in the face with embarrassment and with some consternation I suggested that she get up and drop our case of 78 r.p.m. wax gramophone records onto his lap. If anyone remembers, they presented a pretty hefty load and having done so, she scored a direct hit. He let out a wild scream of pain and fled, doubled-up, into the corridor of the train. We were much relieved by being disencumbered by the attentions of a potential white slave trafficker, although I hoped his prospects for the future in that particular portion of his anatomy were not too bleak.

Having decanted ourselves plus suitcases from the train at Bletchley station, we had to ask a very small boy dressed up as a porter for directions to B.P., as it was known colloquially. He pointed to a rough cinder path and said it was about half a mile away. Weighed down by our luggage like a couple of labourers, we staggered on up the rutted narrow path until on the right side of the track stood an eight-foot high chained fence topped by huge rolls of barbed wire. Further on, the entrance to this barricade was approached by a wide concrete drive with iron gates guarded by soldiers. We presented our passes, which I think at that time just had name and number, and were allowed through after having been given directions to the mansion. As we advanced towards the house of this strange complex it was a bit of a shock, the architecture was the epitome of a Victorian monstrosity with gables; and built of red brick with stone surrounds to the windows. It had to its merit beautiful lawns with a large ornamental lake facing the front elevation. The house was flanked on each side by a series of prefabricated huts. From these quarters emerged assorted males and females wandering in and out, giving the impression of a labyrinth from which there was no exit.

The mystery of what went on in this bewildering enclosure was partially explained to us during an interview with Commander Travis, who was Head of the Station, and which took place as soon as we arrived in the main house. He was a small but good-looking man with a kindly expression and gave us a fairly uninformative talk about the existence and reason for the work here. He declared that the primary purpose was to break the German machine codes, though he was not prepared at this point to elaborate any further. What he did make abundantly clear, however, was that secrecy was of vital importance. We were asked to sign the Official Secrets Act there and then, which, if contravened, would entail imprisonment. He then told us we would be joining Naval Section.

After the retreat from Commander Travis's office, a man for whom I already held in great respect, we were none the wiser as to the function we were to perform in this strange establishment, we decided to do a reconnaissance of the mansion, which somehow did not suit its ostentatious name. The interior was as grotesque as its exterior. The inner hall was spacious with large rooms branching off it, the ceilings had an enrichment of plasterwork which defied description except for looking like a cascade of drooping bosoms; and there did not seem to be any furniture other than a series of trestle tables. On one side of the outer hall hung a large pegboard with a copy of the London *Times* attached to it. There was always a crowd of staff around it at the beginning and end of each shift reading the news and the tragic listings of friends and loved ones killed in action.

We emerged from this eccentric country house armed with instructions as to work schedules; the hours sounded pretty arduous and I felt like a displaced worm in the wrong earth. It was evident that from now on we would use naval expressions only; accordingly, our watches would change weekly and ran as follows, 9-4 p.m. changing to 4 p.m. to midnight the second week and the third week from midnight to 9 a.m. I didn't fancy the last watch at all and wondered how I would keep awake, but I was cheered by the thought of being part of the navy, although puzzled by the absence of all but a few in naval uniform.

Commander Travis had mentioned that Osla and I would be billeted nearby, but as there was nothing available at the moment in a private residence, as a temporary solution we were to be housed in the White Hart Hotel in the market town of Buckingham and transport would be arranged to pick us up at 8 a.m. the next morning.

The hotel, an imposing Neo-Georgian building, looked rather out of place amongst the earlier architecture of the town and had a seedy grandeur about it. The bedroom allotted to us was drab with minimal furnishings. We had not expected luxury, but it did seem a bit sparse. The window overlooked the square, which was a bonus until I discovered that every Sunday morning the Salvation Army band would congregate outside and play rousing marches. On night watch it was a refined form of torture trying to catch a few hours' sleep. However, as yet ignorant of the Sunday decibels, we ate a dinner of overcooked meat with vegetables drowned in saltwater and retired upstairs to console ourselves with music from the gramophone and a new steel needle inserted into the arm piece.

At eight o'clock sharp the following morning a camouflaged car swooped up, driven by a girl in the uniform of the Motor Transport Corps, or M.T.C. as they were called. This Corps performed myriad duties during the war, sometimes dangerous ones, but in this case they would escort us to and from duty watches, a job which they endured in all weathers with the utmost generosity and cheerfulness.

HUT 4, NAVAL SECTION

A part of Naval Section was housed in Hut 4 and truly eponymous, it was a wooden shack close to the mansion consisting of several rooms with concrete floors. I was shown to my place of duty with Osla and several other girls, known as the Index Room. This comprised of a high table with long boxes full of cards with stools to sit on and a narrow shelf upon which to write.

This was it, my introduction to code-breaking, and luckily it did not take me long to find out what I was supposed to do. Decrypted signals translated into English came through to the room in rectangular cardboard boxes, each piece of paper had strips like ticker tape stuck onto them and were teleprinted. I had to pick out the salient points of each signal such as the name of the ship, the captain or harbour master who sent it, the coordinates if any, the recipient and any other pertinent information it contained. All this had to be written on a different card with the appropriate heading, dated and filed. It took me twenty-four hours to realise that I was cross-referencing Top Secret Ultra material, information that very few other than ourselves at Bletchley were allowed to see, let alone know about.

Later on in the war limited access to files and signals were conducted through Special Liaison Units, particularly in the North African Campaign, but for the present Ultra information was given discreetly to field and fleet commanders without any reference to the source. Ultra was the name given to the resulting decryption of all German encoding machines, one of which was Enigma. I often wondered what the ship's captains must have thought when a signal from Admiralty ordered the convoy and escorts to alter course for no apparent reason. Little did they know at the time that Bletchley had deliberately diverted them away from the path of a U-boat wolf pack in mid-Atlantic.

Work in the Index Room at times was boring, a routine job, but it masked information of immense value to the analysts and cryptographers. It was a pity no one told us this, but like everything at Bletchley you had to work it out for yourself. There were rare flashes of insight and interest as to the progress of the war. This rarity was because, when codes were broken, we worked under great pressure and suffered anxiety and tedium when nothing came through to us. I have to confess that during these thankless inactive nights, I would fall asleep on the concrete floor of our cupboard housing the finished indexed signals, but however lowly and monotonous the job was, my ill-informed mind instinctively knew that even at the bottom of the ladder the work was vital.

On-watch people appeared as if in a photograph at a windowed hatch outside the room and would ask, usually in a tearing hurry, if we had a card indicating the movements of a certain ship, place or personnel and go away satisfied when we found the information. I soon realised the true magnitude of a cross-reference index and how it helped to put pieces together like a jigsaw puzzle by interpretation and analysis. It was, in fact, the most comprehensive store of naval intelligence in the country and quite often my memory was jogged by a certain U-boat commander's name. It rang a bell and would fit in with his previous signal to O.K.M., the German Naval Command, giving his precise position in the Atlantic and requesting further orders. This type of signal was very rare because U-boats were usually ordered to keep radio silence. These odd pieces of information seemed to stick in my brain, making it quicker to find the correct card and open up a nearly complete picture of what was required. I had no idea at the time, of course, whether this was a great assistance or not, but our pundits often left the hatch with a smile and a thank you.

There was one very tall naval officer who visited us frequently, called Commander Tandy. He patently thought we were the dregs of the establishment and would bark out his requests as if he was on the quarter deck of a destroyer in action. No show of emotion ever creased his countenance. Some of my kinder hearted colleagues thought it was due to shyness when confronted by decorative-looking girls, I wasn't so sure and we took bets as to who would be the first to make him smile.

THE ENIGMA MACHINE

I should at this point try to relate what actually did take place in this extraordinary and diverse world of Bletchley. I am aware that this has already been written by academics and cryptographical geniuses, but for the untutored and for myself, a single cell in this vast and eclectic organisation, the explanation has to be intelligible and refer only to Naval Intelligence, which I was a part of.

The Enigma machine was invented by the Germans some years before the war and called a Geheimschreiber, meaning "secret writer", possibly they thought it an insurance policy for something, but at some stage they began to manufacture it in Poland and the loyal Poles managed to smuggle one to British Intelligence about the time hostilities began.

The Enigma machine was designed to encipher messages swiftly and thought to be invulnerable to anyone who tried to read the contents. Any book code or one-time pad was considered to be too slow and out of date. The Germans were so smug about this secret form of communication between their Armed Forces on land, sea and air that after the war they were astonished to find that this form of broadcasting their orders and movements had been broken. The answer, had they known it, lay at Bletchley under a blanket of silence for five and a half years.

Intrinsically the Enigma machine was created to baffle any suspect listener by typing messages in German which were then muddled up and could only be made coherent by the receiver who had the means to construe the contents, it transposed the letters in a message from one machine to another. The script was the same length, but instead of being in German it came out as gibberish, unrelated to any known language, and this is what the cryptographers had to contend with once they had received them from our intercept listening Y-stations.

The machine, which I did not catch a glimpse of until well after the war, had adjustable parts which could be set by the operator before transmission of the message. It looked like a typewriter with a keyboard at the front, behind which were three to four rotatable drums connected electrically to the keys. The keyboard was not in any alphabetical order and without numerals, which had to be spelt out in letters, and no punctuation marks.

For the process of encipherment the operator would strike the key he needed at the beginning of the message, it could be a K and end up as a G, but next time he struck a K it would turn out to be a letter other than a K. The mechanical conversion of this process is too technical for me to understand, suffice to say a distorted and unintelligible transcript was the result. This sequence of meaningless letters was then transmitted by wireless telegraphy in Morse code to the recipient, who typed it out on his Enigma machine. Before that, he had to put the parts of his machine in the same order as the sender, I think he had a manual or handbook with instructions to be checked each day at 0001 hours enabling him to read the message in German having reversed the encipherment.

I suppose that today the Enigma machine may sound an easy technological feat, but in the 1940's it was an undisputed triumph of secret communication; that is until Bletchley's cryptographers got hold of its text and unravelled its system, the one that the Germans thought completely unbreakable.

Before any code can be broken it is a simple assumption that it has to be intercepted. This may sound a trivial and obvious statement, but what must be underlined is the magnificent effort put in by the Y-stations all over the country and overseas manned by men and women from all three services. They sat for hours on end listening, glued to their earphones trying to catch the sometimes amphigoric jumble of Morse over the W.T., often made nearly impossible by freak weather conditions or hard-to-locate frequencies. The links between our inland intercept stations and Bletchley were teleprinters and despatch riders. The latter had no idea of the content of their valuable cargo and rode with valour an all weathers, rain, ice or storm. It must at times have been a cheerless job, but their contribution to Ultra was as worthy as that of any other member of Special Intelligence.

To begin with, the cryptographers had the laborious and time-consuming task of trying to match letter for letter in the jumbled text in an effort to make sense of it or try to find a flaw in the code. There were occasional cribs such as daily and routine weather reports from the Luftwaffe airfields and sometimes an operator would always use the same call sign, but it all took a long time until at some point prototype computers were introduced. These machines were called Bombes and were often able to match character for character mechanically, often aided by repetition in signals. Enigma operators were after all human and could make mistakes in transmission, causing the receiver to ask for a repeat. At first these Bombes were lodged in different parts of the country for safety, but eventually most of them landed up at Bletchley and the hut they were lodged in was known as the Hell Hole because of the oil, the dirt and the smell.

The Bombes, when they did arrive, were operated by the W.R.N.S. They were about ten in number, about the size of a very large Victorian wardrobe and ancestors of the modern computers. The pattern of letters or menus sent to them by the cryptographers were fed into the machines by the girls and set up into drums which rotated very fast. This process and servicing was pretty dull for them because they had no idea of what they were doing or why. They must have found it overwhelmingly tedious and long for the end of their watch. The timing of the function that they performed had to be exact and at fifteen-minute intervals the machines stopped, the girls switched off and out of the bottom came a sheet of paper. Armed with this they had to run the length of the room and hand it to the W.R.E.N. officer in charge of the watch, who in turn despatched it to the cryptographers in Hut 6.

If Hut 6 had guessed the menus and sequence even remotely right the transmission was broken, but by this time some of the signals, although in German, were often mixed up or corrupt with words joined together due to weak signal strengths or bad weather conditions. The highly intelligent and skilled staff of the Z Room in Naval Section, which was manned like us all in watches twenty-four hours a day and were experts in languages, received the appropriate decrypts. They then proceeded to make sense of the inglorious muddle after which the head of the watch evaluated the texts before handing them off to the translators, who in turn passed them on to the Index Room for filing. If the information in the signal warranted immediate attention he would pass a copy to the War Cabinet, but mark it as an assessment with no comment because it was not Bletchley's job to make strategical decisions but to provide information.

I should apologise for the paucity of my description of the Enigma, also to the cryptanalysts and other great brains at Bletchley who helped save our lives. This is not their story alone, but also of the young girls who were carried away unknowingly into the talented and obscure world of Special Intelligence, of how they lived, loved and survived, and never breathed so much as a word about their work. They were a credit to the security of the nation and for nearly fifty years none of us revealed the immense value of the job we did for so long in a world that only a chosen few knew about. It is an example for today to certain people who seem incapable of keeping their mouths shut. I refer, of course, to the author of that exceedingly bad book *Spycatcher*.

KEEPING THE SECRET SAFE

There have been some books written about Ultra, unfortunately without the benefit of esoteric knowledge of its workings. These tomes did a great deal of damage and unnecessarily upset people after the war who had lost loved ones believing that Ultra had too zealously guarded its source and left them unprotected. The truth was that Bletchley could not always decipher signals when code words were used in transmissions from the Luftwaffe, such as the ones regarding the raid on Coventry. It was impossible to guess which city was to be bombed. We knew the date and the approximate time, but which one defeated the code-breakers in Hut 3. Each city had been given a code name, Coventry came through as Korn and it was only the brilliance of Professor R. V. Jones who bent the radio beams of the enemy aircraft that gave us a fix on the city, but alas it was too late and the dreadful devastation took place.

On the subject of security, I had been at Bletchley about three months when some good soul thought it an excellent idea to give us some lectures on the need for silence regarding Ultra material. As it had never occurred to any one of us to breathe a word about our work, we thought it hilariously funny and a bit late in the day. We all duly attended the sessions, found them singularly uneducative and giggled throughout most of them. It seemed to me quite superfluous, having signed the Official Secrets Act, to then be taught how to obey it. The Armed Forces were naturally reticent as to what they were doing, whether it was a proposed bombing raid, firing from a tank or digging trenches somewhere abroad, but Osla and I had already thought up a good cover story because all our friends away from B.P. wanted to know what we were doing buried away somewhere in the depths of the country.

When on leave and in London amongst friends, the conversations ranged from the latest love affairs to the type and purpose of your employment, exciting or dull; payment never came into it, none of us received much money whatever the job. In fact there were times when it was a struggle to find the cash for a train journey up to London after having paid your billeting dues. As days off were so precious and time so short, I usually took the milk train from Euston back to Bletchley at five o'clock in the morning, arriving in time for the 9 a.m. watch, a bit bleary-eyed and hoping the head of the watch would find my work satisfactory and not notice I was a touch overdressed from a night on the town. We thought it awfully smart to have a hangover, a pretty childish fantasy since we only drank something very distantly related to orange juice.

So, it happened one evening in London that Osla and I were put to the test and were seriously questioned about what we did. The talk had revolved round our girl friends' activities and they were quick to tell us what glamorous jobs they had. The first girl declared with bright eyes and great emphasis, "I am the personal assistant to the admiral in charge of the docks at Portsmouth." Well, bully for you, I thought, trying to ignore her smirk. Another, eager to impart her important contribution to the war effort, said, "I drive a four-star American general in a real Cadillac and what's more there is a gun in the back." This was followed by the next girl who could hardly contain her impatience and unconcealed pride when she said, "Well, I am the aide to someone very high up in the War Office." This was getting too much for Osla and I, who could hardly counter with "My dears, the U-boats we sink." But we had come prepared because, after much thought and previous rehearsal, we had decided to begin with the sentence certain to enthral: "It's a secret, promise not to tell?" Having captivated our audience and certain to have grabbed their total concentration, we proceeded in dramatic tones and with renewed requests for discretion to explain in detail that we kept files on those who were to receive medals for valour in the field of battle. We managed to talk long enough on the subject to produce looks of glazed boredom on the faces of our interrogators, who begged us not to continue. We had succeeded in gaining a reputation for being extremely prosaic, pitied for doing such a routine job and never questioned again. It appeared that word had gone round that it was a mistake to ask Sarah and Osla about their work because they bored you to tears with their childish enthusiasm.

Security had its comical as well as its serious side at times. Colonel Stewart Menzies was our boss, our hero. Head of MI6 and Special Intelligence, he was an amazing man with a shrewd and brilliant brain. This talent he managed to totally disguise with the bearing of a Guards officer, feigning disinterest in anything but regimental matters. He fooled everybody outside the intelligence organisations and even after the war very few knew what a vital role he played. One evening he and his wife were dining with my mother, and as they were old friends she confided in him that she was worried about me because she had no idea where I was other than a Post Office number, and furthermore had no notion what I did. He was very sympathetic about her anxiety but doubted he could help in any way because, after all, he was only a Colonel in a Guards Regiment. He did add, however, that anyone with a P.O. Box number must be doing a good job, which probably left her more confused than before.

Other than a few bouts of levity, which we were all guilty of, I only got into big trouble once, which was not my fault. One morning, working as usual in the Index Room, I heard many footsteps outside then the door opened and in walked my godfather. At that time he was Vice Admiral, Lord Louis Mountbatten, Chief of Combined Operations and naturally privy to Ultra. He was accompanied by a lot of Top Brass and harassed-looking Bletchley staff. I managed to splutter in my astonishment, "Uncle Dickie, what are you doing here?"

"Oh," he said, "I knew you were here and thought I would see how you are getting on; show me the system of your cross-reference index."

Pink with embarrassment I showed him, conscious of the waves of anger behind from the learned code-breakers. The gross error for which I was not guilty was that a visit to the Index was not on the programme and the chronology planned minute by minute was put off course.

I was awfully pleased to see Uncle Dickie and, as the Index was considered fairly lowly work, all of us on watch were thrilled. Doom descended the next morning with a peremptory demand to see Commander Travis forthwith. He asked me how I had dared to ask the Chief of Combined Ops to visit the Index. I assured him, eyes full of tears, that I knew nothing about the visit and that he was my godfather. He believed that I spoke the truth and, bless him, lent me a hankie to blow my nose.

Security, of course, had proliferated well beyond the bounds of Station X, the whole of Britain was conscious of its importance. Motor cars had to be made secure, not that Osla and I had one. Victor had long since bitten the dust, but my mother's little Morris Minor had to be fitted with the correct precautions in line with the blackout regulations. Headlamps had to have a slit mask, dimmed sidelights, and only a glimmer was permitted on the indicators, which stuck out like an arm and were operated by a switch from inside the vehicle. This was quite a new advance in comfort and saved one from arm gestures through an open window. Reversing lights were prohibited and matt paint had to be applied to the rear bumper for fear the chrome might reflect, but most important of all, when leaving the car at night you had to disable it by removing the rotor arm in case a German popped in and stole it.

In cities and small towns posters proliferated. All exhorted us to be careful what we said in public, like "Careless Talk Costs Lives", and one particularly silly one like "Tittle-Tattle Lost The Battle". We had spy mania and any unfortunate person with a foreign accent, blond hair and a thick neck was automatically suspect. There was one story which I cannot verify but worth the telling about a stationmaster at a small rail halt on the north-east coast of Scotland. It boasted one train a day, which did not qualify for a large staff. Early one morning at his ticket window appeared two strangers. That in itself caused distrust, war or no war. He was used to the odd shepherd with three sheep, but the ultimate suspicion fell when these two men, curt of speech, handed him two white five pound notes and asked for tickets to a town not ten miles away, that was it! No one had ever given him such a large sum for such a short journey and he decided they were German spies recently landed by U-boat. He let them go their way and called the local constabulary by one of those old telephones that worked only by cranking a handle with great force. They were caught and imprisoned as enemy agents. It didn't say much for the briefing by their spy masters.

A NEW BILLET

At last the sleepless days on night watch in the town of Buckingham came to an end and Osla and I were moved to a permanent billet.

It was a beautiful house of the Queen Anne period in a village nearby owned by an elderly couple who were very good to us. They already had two people from Bletchley, a quiet gentle lady and a grumpy-looking professor from Cambridge. It had quite a long drive, which meant a fair sprint in the early morning to catch the transport. None of the drivers could wait because they had other people to pick up. Osla, who had difficulty in waking up, even with my short-tempered shouts and shakes, used to catch the car by the skin of her teeth. One morning she missed it completely. I thought that might teach her a lesson, but to my fury she arrived at Bletchley before us, having hitched a ride in a Rolls-Royce.

In the house we had a two bedded room, a shared bathroom and a small sitting room in the attic. In comparison to the hotel in Buckingham it was paradise. The large garden was unattended except for vegetables and in the summer the grass grew so long you could sunbathe topless without being seen. My memories of the bedroom are split between the seasons. The comfort and peace were combined with the perishing cold of a winter's morning. We had a small one-bar electric fire of much reduced power. It presented the conundrum of whether to leap out of bed ten minutes early to switch on the doubtful warmth and watch your knickers and bra hopefully heating, or to sleep away those precious minutes and thus committing oneself to iced underwear.

Other than the quiet middle-aged lady who wouldn't say boo to a goose, our other lodger along the corridor was the Professor of Philosophy from King's College, Cambridge. Most of our scholars came from that university. We found him to be pompous and positively ancient. He was neither, but he did suffer from a total lack of humour which was probably due to the propinquity of such lighthearted girls, the like of which he had obviously never encountered before. As impudent young brats you tended to categorise people unfairly. Possibly he was wanting in understanding, but the little he may have had must have been stretched to the limit by our naughty tricks.

We teased him constantly, which his academic mind could not comprehend. The final villainy we played upon him was in retrospect rather unkind. We hid the wind-up gramophone under his bed one evening with the starter handle attached to a long piece of string snaking through the passage to our bedroom. At midnight we pulled it and the poor man was violently awoken by the strains of Beethoven's Ninth Symphony. As a result he begged to change billets and was kind enough not to blame us. We truly missed him and were temporarily conscience-stricken.

Our love life had its ups and downs, the highs and lows both ever magnified, either enraptured or suicidal. I got engaged to a handsome officer in the Coldstream Guards, but was soon disengaged by both families who thought we were too young and, anyway, it was wartime. What that had to do with it escaped me, but my heart was broken for the first time. I felt I would never survive the anguish and, when he was killed in France, the misery was compounded. Osla also suffered. She promised to marry a diplomat and came back to Bletchley from leave sporting a large emerald ring on her left hand; but two months later the despicable cad changed his mind. Poor Osla tearfully returned the ring, swearing she had never liked green stones anyway.

Being temporarily loveless, we decided that hearts in bits and pieces should for the moment be ignored in favour of improving the mind. It was time to concentrate on the intellect off duty as well as on. This decision led Osla to further her education in modern Greek from an old book she found somewhere and I did the same with Russian, which was almost as difficult. We sat at each end of our cold sitting room emitting strange noises in an effort to master the puzzling alphabets.

I found Russian particularly hard. It is an East Slavonic language with thirty-two letters in the alphabet and all those mysterious-looking letters which left me wondering why a B should be pronounced as a V, but I felt it should be conquered so as to further my post-war career as a foreign correspondent and for a while all seemed to go well, boosting my confidence in multi-linguistic capabilities. It was not until much later on after I had been sent up to work at Admiralty that I decided to polish up the language a bit and took lessons from a Russian lady. She hooted with laughter as I spoke and told me I had been putting the emphasis and accent on the wrong syllables, which took weeks to correct when off duty. No wonder wireless broadcasts from the Soviet Union sounded strange, and what complicated the future was that I was being taught Imperial Russian rather than the vocabulary of Stalin.

The comfort of our new billet was making life much easier for us and Osla's appetite was much assuaged by the housekeeper, who managed to cook potatoes in so many different ways it was a joy to eat them. The rationing of soap caused a few tiffs between us. We were only allowed 2 oz. of toilet bars or flakes per month, therefore we were constantly accusing each other of purloining bits as they got smaller and thinner. Other than these minor spats we got on prodigiously well and valued each other's company as we always had.

There were of course other matters to concern us rather than squabbling over slivers of soap. Soon after Osla and I arrived at Bletchley came the horrific news that the German battleships *Scharnhorst, Gneisenau* and the *Prinz Eugen* had left the port of Brest in north-west France and in broad daylight had cruised through the English Channel to reach Wilhelmshaven in north Germany. We were rendered speechless by the impertinence of such an action, but Commander Denning at Operational Intelligence Centre in Admiralty had already sent his assessment to the chiefs of staff saying that such an operation might be feasible. He reckoned that although Grand Admiral Erich Raeder would have preferred the northern route south of Iceland, Hitler, in one of his displays of manic clairvoyance, ordered the quickest approach to the east because he was convinced the British would invade Norway and he would need all his naval armament to stop us.

There were all kinds of complex and awkward reasons for these great ships being able to sail under our noses to their destination. Ultra did not seem to have played any part in the story with the exception of Denning's brilliant analysis, which could not have been taken seriously enough. They did not exactly get away with it unscathed however; R.A.F. fighter sweeps had been alerted and spotted the ships off the mouth of the Somme. Having escaped detection for eleven hours, *Scharnhorst* and *Gneisenau* hit magnetic mines laid by Bomber Command and *Prinz Eugen* suffered minor damage. The ships

limped into Wilhelmshaven to be out of action for several
months.

VISITORS AND ECCENTRICS

Within the confines of Bletchley Park we had more bad news. Admiral Karl Dönitz was in command of all U-boats. He introduced a new Enigma cipher called Triton, later known as Shark. It was to be used for Atlantic operations only and directly linked to Dönitz in Paris. He might have had a suspicion that we were reading his transmissions, which was never proved, but he added an extra rotor to the three previously on the Enigma machine. Up till then it had been using the Hydra code, which we had already broken. Our cryptographers and the Bombes were unable to crack Shark for eleven agonising months from February to December 1942. During that time it left our shipping in the Atlantic open to be preyed upon by U-boats. We lost a devastating amount of shipping and lives and it was immensely difficult to know how to reroute convoys.

Despite our depression, some happenings cheered us up. We began to have some very important visitors, people prominent in their particular field and therefore of great interest in our enclosed world. It was a visible compensation for all our hard work and their evident appreciation was quite a tonic. Some of them seemed astonished and struck numb by Bletchley's achievements. Although these visitors were few and far between, with the exception of our beloved C. there was one man who, as far as I know, came but once, but that was enough. It was the Prime Minister, Winston Churchill, and I was lucky enough to be on duty. He stood on a soapbox outside the ugly mansion exuding power and confidence, surrounded by all those staff who were able to leave their work. The sun shone and he waited a few minutes whilst we shuffled about angling for position; then he lifted his head and said, "To look at you, one would not think you held so many secrets, but I know better and I am proud of you." If he said anything else I have forgotten it, but those first words were an inspiration to us all and influenced me to the end of the war. It was the praise and appreciation that was our only reward; it was all the thanks we needed and it was all the thanks we got.

Looking back to V.E. Day on 8th May 1945 and V.J. Day on 2nd September of that same year, reliving the happiness and relief that the conflict was over, I remember a feeling of being forgotten — no campaign ribbons, not that we deserved any, no certificate such as our colleagues in the Red Cross received. Just nothing — even a pat on the back might have elevated the psyche, but then if you work for Special Intelligence that's what you must expect and on reflection it was well worth it.

I became very much aware of certain cryptographers and cryptanalysts, mainly because of their undisputed genius, but also due to their amazing habits and eccentricities. I wished so much to be friendly with Professor Alan Turing, possibly our greatest mathematician and inventor of the Bombe. My wish was never really granted. I once offered him a cup of tea but he shrank back in fear. He seemed terrified of girls and on the rare occasions when he was spotted like a protected species, he would be shambling down to the canteen in a curious sideways step, his eyes fixed to the ground. It was explained to me that if you had spent most of your adult life closeted away in a study at Cambridge, you too would be scared of women and not know how to handle them.

His wayward eccentricity was delightful, if occasionally bizarre, and seemed to enhance his personality. I think he must have suffered from hay fever because during the summer months he would bicycle to work from his billet wearing a gas mask, it was the only interpretation I could think of for wanting to breathe through the heat and discomfort of such a contraption. This particular bicycle was the source of great amusement to us; apparently the chain was faulty and he refused to have it mended because it gave him pleasure to count the number of times the pedals went round before reaching the break. The calculation completed, he would get off the machine and adjust the chain. Alas, his homosexuality, which was never apparent, was to lead to his suicide after the war; his death, due to a series of unfortunate incidents displaying considerable naivete, was a tragic end to one of our greatest mathematicians and he died relatively unknown.

Another giant of pure mathematics was a tall man called Professor Alan Ross. He had a long red beard and hair to match. In the winter on particularly cold and frosty days he wore a pale blue pixie-like hood over his beard tied round his chin to protect it from the icy winds and presented a very droll sight. He also taught himself Japanese as a relaxation when off duty — the brain potential was such that few could achieve those powerful heights. Talking of eccentricity, a friend told me she saw Angus Wilson, the famous writer, throw himself into the lake in a tantrum and had to be pulled out.

There was a story going round within the confines of Bletchley about the end of 1942 that was weird, but totally believable at the time. Two young submariners who had been patrolling the North Atlantic for some time being constantly bombarded by enemy torpedoes, deafened by depth charges underwater in an effort to protect our vital shipping lanes, were physically and probably mentally worn out. Admiralty, in its infinite wisdom, decided that they needed rest followed by a spell of shore duty.

They were ordered to report to Naval Section, Station X at Bletchley. This command was sent to them with the usual uncommunicative bluntness which must have caused them some concern. On the appointed day they approached B.P. up the narrow cinder path from the railway station, immaculately dressed, but grey with fatigue. They then spotted the huge rolls of barbed wire, further on a squad of Military Police and within a compound, an assortment of strange-looking human beings. These two poor sailors, having survived the terrible harshness of the Atlantic, were quite reasonably overcome by panic. The thought struck them immediately that they had been sent to a lunatic asylum, the result of too many months at sea. They fled back to the station where one of them stole a bicycle and got to the port of Dover. The other stowed away on the next train and escaped to the north of Scotland. It was several days before they were retrieved and gently persuaded to return. No one was particularly surprised by these turn of events because from the outside looking in we must have seemed a motley crowd of chattering cretins and the escapade was never referred to again.

Bletchley was now growing, with many more people recruited to help as the German signal traffic increased. We had to move from our Hut 4 to a large concrete building next to the lake called Block B. We didn't like it at all, it seemed so stark after the cosiness of the old quarters and perversely continued to be called Hut 4. I must admit it had more space, but we still enjoyed grumbling, and rightly nobody paid any attention to us.

PROMOTION

I seemed to be growing out of the Index Room like a child whose socks have shrunk. The job had become relatively easy and an almost mechanical procedure which I was beginning to find boring, repetitive, and I felt I needed to be stretched further. Fortune was with me; with an increased knowledge of plain and technical German I was transferred to a vastly more interesting job, which was to translate the decrypted signals from German into English. Some of the signals, although plenty had passed through my hands in the Index, were methodological and difficult to understand at first, but I refused to admit hardship and battled through, determined to secure my promotion and the added spur was a small rise in salary. The girls I worked with were familiar with the vernacular and therefore more qualified than I, on paper that is, and with university degrees in the language were paid more, but I had one advantage which was my fluency in German and to hell with the grammar.

My peers in this office taught me a lot; in fact, they taught me how to think, to question facts and literature. We had amazing conversations during the quieter hours, particularly on the subject of philosophy, about which I knew next to nothing. There were long arguments as to the true meaning of tragedy. I thought it meant losing a loved one in an accident, but no, college minds insisted that true tragedy was self-inflicted. We debated the theories of Ludwig Feuerbach. We also discussed the problems of another German philosopher, Friedrich Nietzsche, who sounded pretty potty to me. He had rejected Christianity and moral values. Possibly ill health had warped his mind. He was influenced by Wagner, whom he was close to, but obsessed by his domineering sister who was engrossed in keeping the purity of the Teutonic race and wanted him to join her in a remote part of South America. Despite his totalitarian views he refused the offer of an undefiled life in the Brazilian jungle and spent his later years in northern Italy.

All this wisdom, knowledge and analysis from the academic world was mind-boggling to me, but there were comic moments when one graduate of philosophy pronounced that Kierkegaard the Danish thinker, for all his theories, was really in love with his mother's umbrella.

Having after a time established that I could cope with the translations of all signals, I found a lot of the work was routine. There were of course some decrypts of great advantage and excitement, but the exhilaration was sometimes dampened by not being able to use the priceless material and its information. The reason for this negative state was the fear of prejudicing the source. This was an all-important and vital rule and the decision to employ it or not rested with the Prime Minister and the chiefs of staff. It was crystal clear to us at B.P. that if the Germans ever suspected that we had penetrated their ciphers, "Ultra, the goose that laid the golden eggs" (to use Churchill's expression) was dead and buried and we would probably lose the war.

Keeping these secrets to ourselves led to much heartache and sorrow. I can remember instances in the early days of the horrifying U-boat attacks on our convoys and merchant vessels in the Atlantic who were bringing us much needed food and ammunition. Frequently the convoys had to be told to "scatter." This left the merchant ships without the protection of the naval frigates and destroyers, leaving them defenceless and clear targets for enemy torpedoes. Unless it could be proved that the U-boats had been spotted from the air by R.A.F. reconnaissance, in which case the convoy would be told to alter route and navigate away from the wolf pack, Admiral Dönitz would have been instantly aware that something was very wrong with their transmissions and lead him to be concerned about their machine codes being broken. True enough, they remained convinced that Enigma was unbreakable, but the result of any suspicion would have proved a disaster for Ultra.

The same misery, loss of life and ships was later experienced on the route to Archangel in northern Russia through the icy, treacherous waters of the North Sea and the Arctic Circle; but this time it was not due to the protection of Ultra, but a disbelieving mind in Admiralty. In July 1942, a large convoy named PQ 17 was directed from somewhere near Iceland to Murmansk; it was carrying supplies to Russia. She was escorted by ships of the British Home Fleet and comprised of thirty-four merchant ships. It was a very dangerous mission because the great German battleship *Tirpitz* was lurking in Altenfjord in Norway, and in other northern fjords the known presence of a powerful enemy striking force consisting of two pocket battleships, a heavy cruiser and a destroyer group. The Home Fleet could have protected the convoy off the North Cape, except for the immense and deadly power of the *Tirpitz*. Would she or would she not sail to attack?

The First Sea Lord, Admiral Sir Dudley Pound, consulted Commander Denning, Chief of Operational Intelligence in the Citadel located underneath Admiralty. From Denning's analysis and appreciation of Ultra decrypts, he could only give Admiral Pound negative rather than positive information. The *Tirpitz* had not yet sailed but at any moment she could; but not before her destroyer escort and air reconnaissance had been sent out ahead to clear the way of mines and other shipping. This would have involved a lot of wireless traffic; so far there had been none. Commander Denning's shrewd assessment had proved correct, for *Tirpitz* remained snugly in Altenfjord. Alas, Admiral Pound did not heed the advice of the intelligence analysts. Believing the battleship would sail, he ordered the escorting cruiser squadron to withdraw and the convoy to "scatter." The result was a tragedy, an appalling loss of life as merchant ships were blown out of the water by German U-boats and the Luftwaffe, a dreadful tally of twenty-three ships sunk. It would be impertinent of me to criticise Admiral Pound for not trusting Ultra, but in my experience for the first few years of the war many admirals were equally untrusting.

I have tried to give examples of how Ultra had to be protected and how the assessments were often treated with scepticism. After the thirty years when the prohibitive silence of Ultra was lifted by the Official Secrets Act, fortunately the truth has been chronicled by esoteric authors who worked at Bletchley. Many must have wept for years wondering why British Intelligence had let them down in their hour of greatest need.

MISCHIEF AND HIGH JINKS

We thought a lot about food. There is a saying that an army marches on its stomach and most of us were convinced we belonged to that order of things. Night watches were especially vulnerable to rumbling tummies and usually forced us to go down to the canteen at about three a.m. where the food was indescribably awful. It is a well-known fact that to cater for so many people is difficult and particularly in wartime; however, given the raw ingredients palatability need not be ignored, but our canteen outshone any sleazy restaurant in producing sludge and the smell of watery cabbage and stale fat regularly afflicted the nostrils to the point of nausea.

One night I found a cooked cockroach nestling in my meat, if you can dignify it by that name, the meat not the beetle. I was about to return the offending object to the catering manageress, when Osla, who had the appetite of a lioness with cubs, snatched the plate and said, "What a waste, I'll eat round it." How she managed to eat so much minus the insect and stay so slim I never knew, because any leftovers on any nearby plate were gobbled up by her in a flash.

There were a few naval officers in our section, too few for my liking. Curiously enough Admiralty was considered a civilian organisation and as civilians we were paid by the Foreign Office, even though we worked for the navy. I dreamed about being taken out by one of this rare uniformed breed and this wish occasionally came true. The Mecca establishment for an outing was a pub in Stony Stratford a few miles down the road. It did involve, however, doing a Cinderella act at midnight in time to catch the twelve o'clock transport back to my billet. Romance never blossomed alas, except almost once; he was a tall, dark, handsome sailor with beguiling grey eyes and a scholar of some repute.

I had become something of an intellectual snob by then, aroused by the eclectic conversations of my peers. The combination of good looks and brains in this Adonis was perfect and I lived in a haze of romantic idealism. He wrote me affectionate poems in Russian and always used the diminutive of my name, it was the epitome of enchantment and I waited for his letters via the internal postal system with undisguised impatient indulgence. Unhappily, I don't think he really fancied me. It was just the idea of being in love; nevertheless I shall always remember him as one who brought exceptional talents and gifts into my life.

Amongst my many friends in this unique world was a larger-than-life girl called Jean, she later became Baroness Trumpington and a great Parliamentarian. We all loved her. She never appeared without a smile on her face; you couldn't rub it off, however bad the news was. She had an incredible sense of fun, and this quality, which we all enjoyed, did much to discomfort our immediate boss, newly arrived at Station X. He was a lanky young man with a permanently morose expression due, I suppose, to the impossible task of keeping us in order and stopping the irrepressible laughter which rang through the passage during our short breaks. I don't think he understood that because we worked so hard, a few high jinks were the only way we could unwind and our playpen was very small.

At some time I had managed to smuggle in an electric cooker ring. We hid it in the signals cupboard which had an appropriate socket. What demented architect had put it there we knew not, except perhaps for the convenience of burning papers in the event of an invasion. In any case it was tremendously useful to stave off hunger pangs during the long watches of the night, but one evening during a brew up and whilst dangling a bit of bread over the heat, our vengeful master came steaming into the room shouting at the top of his strident voice. "I smell toast, who is responsible for this outrage?" Having just managed to close the door to hide the offending object, Jean, to her eternal credit, stood up and said, "But I always smell of toast." We got away with that particular incident, but a later event drove him into an excess of fury which was not easy to calm down, although his rage was diminished by the sheer weight of numbers of miscreants.

Our new concrete building had a long wide corridor with all the rooms off it and ended in a T-junction. One afternoon after a 9-4 watch and before transport was ready, we decided that Jean would like a ride in a large laundry basket normally used to move secret files. Nothing loth she climbed willingly into it, the basket was propelled by castor wheels and we launched it down the long stretch of corridor, where it gathered momentum by the second. Like hounds after a hare we tried to gain on the rectangular rocket, when to our horror at the T-junction Jean suddenly disappeared, basket and all, through some double swing doors, crashing to a halt inside the men's toilets. History does not relate the feelings of the occupants and Jean was giggling too much to notice. A true gentleman must have pushed her out for she reappeared within a minute still in the basket and quite unabashed.

Now trouble was brewing. A very serious reprimand was administered and watches changed so that we were distributed amongst a more sober group. This fortunately did not last long and we managed to reform our team. This was mainly allowed because the work we achieved was considered very satisfactory and we wore repentant expressions. Our wretched young boss had had enough and shortly afterwards requested a transfer to another section. I suspected he pleaded secondment to be as far away as possible from the terrors of Naval Section.

I had always thought that some of our minor internal escapades were overlooked because the head of Hut 4 was a marvellous man called Frank Birch. He was a Fellow of King's College, Cambridge, the university that gave birth to much of our mathematical strength. He also loved acting in the theatre and was renowned for his performances as Widow Twanky in the pantomime *Aladdin*. It was his great sense of humour which possibly allowed him to forgive our lesser irresponsible acts. You didn't often get a laugh from signals, but occasionally we would get transmissions from Admiralty, they were usually about floating or acoustic mines that we might be able to shed some light on. One night a pink slip came through, I presume by mistake, from the duty officer in the Citadel regarding a convoy which read, "Gracie Fields making water." This referred of course to a merchant ship which had been torpedoed. I am ashamed to say it had us all rolling on the floor with laughter but at the same time wishing her crew a safe rescue.

CODES AND CIPHERS

My part in the Ultra story is written from memory. Woe betide anyone at Bletchley who kept a diary, even a social one. I hope my memory does not let me down and provide encouragement to fall into the trap of romancing the life we led. It is also important to tell the story as I knew it then and not within the light of mature retrospection and hindsight. I am well aware stories get better for the telling.

I began to comprehend when I started to translate the decrypts that within the vast amount of traffic in radio signals that Ultra gathered into its cocoon were some transmissions from Hitler. He had a mania for conducting campaigns himself; directives flowed from the Führer to the O.K.W., the High Command of the German Armed Services and to O.K.M., the High Command of all German Naval Forces. This must have been very awkward for them as he was ill-briefed and frequently wrong. We began to acquire an enormous and comprehensive output of information gathered with glee by our cryptographers and analysts and sometimes received with suspicion and disbelief by those who needed it most.

Before I arrived at Bletchley a benefit of immense good fortune came to the code-breakers. In May 1941 the U-boat 110 was captured off the coast of Greenland with her Enigma machine and all cipher material intact by one of our destroyers, H.M.S. *Bulldog*. The escort corvette *Aubretia* had picked her up on firm Asdic contact and dropped ten depth charges and the U-boat surfaced. Captain Baker-Cresswell, having lost two ships in his convoy, was about to ram her but changed his mind. German crew were by then on deck and preparing to man their gun, so *Bulldog* opened fire with all weapons, killing the captain. The survivors were put below decks on *Aubretia* and 110 was taken in tow and subsequently sank. This was not before Sub. Lt. Balme was left aboard to guard the U-boat. Unaware whether the German captain had set the destructive explosives, he had to stay for a whole hour before *Bulldog* returned from orders to search for another U-boat. Back at Bletchley one of our most trusted and valuable men in the shape of a dazzlingly good-looking sailor, Commander Alan Bacon, was despatched to Scapa Flow to bring back the priceless cargo. It was fortunate perhaps that U-110 sank, therefore causing no anxiety to Admiral Dönitz, who would have been greatly concerned had he known about his lost ciphers. It was hoped that he concluded the U-boat had been depth charged and immediately sunk without reporting the attack.

The result of this treasure trove enabled Bletchley to read the U-boat traffic within forty-eight hours of reception, evaluate it together with the existing knowledge of the German Air Force codes and reports from British agents and other sources. This cipher was called Hydra and was used by all enemy submarines in the Atlantic.

Gossip and exchange of information was permissible within Hut 4, Naval Section, as long as it did not go any further. It did help one psychologically to know a few bits of exoteric news, good or bad, to enliven the atmosphere. The chewing of the stubby pencil over seemingly endless routine decrypts and the pressure of work did not always allow time to put two and two together, but it was from this internal grapevine that I first heard about Shark and the deadlock in breaking it. The breaking of this perplexing code did not come until December 1942, during which time our shipping losses grew alarmingly.

This cipher was being used and directly linked to Admiral Dönitz in Paris, and left us, forgive the pun, all at sea.

For all those months Bletchley worked on, aware that vital supplies as well as ships and lives were being lost day and night. The exceptions to the toll of casualties were the cruise liners S.S. *Queen Elizabeth* and the S.S. *Queen Mary*, which were used as troop carriers. They were too fast for submarine attack and if they maintained a zigzag course they were safe from torpedoes. The solution was so near and yet so far. We could only estimate the positions of the underwater assassins; I use the word "we" advisedly and with caution, for it was not myself, three blondes, two brunettes and a redhead in the Translation Section who had to work at full power to solve the conundrum, but the blistering intellect of the occupants of Hut 8.

This lack of essential knowledge of the exact German U-boat positions in the Atlantic was tantalizing as well as deadly serious. The existing patterns of U-boat behaviour presented by Hydra were the only resources Admiralty had at the time, minimal though they were, and came through largely due to those in Operational Intelligence. Amongst them and *primus inter pares* was an exceptional R.N.V.R. officer called Rodger Winn, a man of astuteness and logic unparalleled. He had the capacity to guess, usually correctly, the positions of enemy shipping in the Atlantic. It was almost as if he could read the mind of Admiral Dönitz. Rodger Winn was a remote star to me, but his brilliant assessments were well-known within Hut 4 and Hut 8.

At last, in December 1942, Shark was broken, an almost unbelievable achievement on the part of our cryptographers. You could see the relief on the faces of all those in Hut 4. The flood of decrypts was about to burst upon us like a broken dam and we were eager to get on with it.

Without this super-human feat, Hitler may well have won the war, crippling and starving us of food and weapons by the deadly power of his iron-clad sharks who could roam the seas undetected. The torturing months of the brave convoy escorts and merchant ships were nearly over. Now it was our duty to give them intelligence cover from Ultra's sources without guesswork. A staggering load of work began, every decrypt was analysed, assessed, translated and filed in the mighty Cross-Reference Index, whether vital or routine. There were few days off that December and nobody complained.

In Naval Section all decrypts after having been checked by the watchkeeper on duty, translated into English, were presumably copied and sent to the Operational Intelligence Centre in Admiralty. They were always prefaced by the letter Z, these letters ranged in degree of priority up to ZZZZZ, but if the eventual recipient of the signal was not authorised to receive Ultra, or Top Secret U as it was usually called, then the text would end with the words, "Admiralty Appreciation." A nice little security touch.

ECLECTIC MEMORIES

Sometimes the railway became the carriers of Ultra material, which I discovered to be a rather perilous and insecure form of transportation. On one occasion when I was travelling up to London on leave, I was forced to stand in the Guard's van due to serious overcrowding, when I spotted to my horror a Bletchley bag unaccompanied in one corner; there was an odd assortment of passengers standing alongside me, most of them grey with fatigue and resignation, but in my distress I was convinced that most of them were enemy agents. Alarmed and shaking at the consequence of it being stolen I sat on it for the rest of the journey to Euston and was extremely reluctant to release it even to the Military Police who came to fetch it. On my return from leave I mentioned this unfortunate episode to the head of Naval Section, but I could not tell from the look on his face whether he was disturbed by this or not. Whatever his opinion, in true Bletchley tradition, he was not going to tell me.

Security and silence reigned within this secret establishment. I knew that the naval scientific cryptographers were in Hut 8 and in Hut 4 where I worked was the centre for analysing and processing the intelligence they provided. Other than that I had no awareness nor any desire to know what those in other huts did; it was frowned upon to fraternise. This seemed quite normal to me and we had been trained not to be inquisitive; however, there were a few exceptions to this rule I had several friends whom I used to meet up with in the canteen who worked in the army huts. If I wanted to know the whereabouts and positions of certain regiments in which I had a special interest, fraternal and love interest being predominate, they would be happy to tell me. These girls, besides having knowledge of German Army movements, also knew the actions of our own forces. They would give me the information knowing there would be an undercover return service from Naval Section.

I once did a favour for a girl from one of the air force huts. She had a boyfriend in the navy who was serving in a cruiser in the Far Eastern Fleet; she had not received any news from him for two months and was concerned for his safety. Having been given the name of his ship and with help from a friend in Admiralty it was not difficult for me to get the relevant information regarding his whereabouts. The news was not what she wanted to hear — the roguish sailor had been based at Trincomalee off the East Indian coast for two months awaiting replacement and damage repairs. I was not surprised to see the sadness on her face on receipt of this communication, but the surprise was his to come and a lesson learnt. He returned in due course with stories of weeks spent at sea, unable to post letters and other fancy tales. He was totally rejected by her without a word of explanation. The moral of this narrative is if you are going to tell lies to a girlfriend, never do it to one in the intelligence services (but then he wasn't to know that). I knew that these internal exchanges of information were very much discouraged, but I never got caught and kept my mouth firmly shut on the subject.

As late as December 1940 there was always a threat of invasion. We knew this was a possibility due to the ravings of Hitler and his determination to cross the Channel; also from the successes that Bletchley had attained in breaking the German Air Force code, although the naval codes were still a problem, at least through the G.A.F. codes, to accomplish a successful invasion of Britain. No fleet of ships and army personnel could move without air cover, so this involved a great deal of wireless air traffic which we were reading as fast as the Enigma operator could transmit it.

By the time Osla and I had arrived at Bletchley the danger seemed to be over, but I did sometimes wonder what we should do if it ever happened. It occurred to me that as we were not in uniform and were salaried by the Foreign Office, we civilian staff would not be covered by the Geneva Convention, which protected prisoners of war, and reports from British agents as to the comforts of the German camps were chilling. It was uncomfortable food for thought. I supposed we would have to have an enormous bonfire of signals and run for our lives to avoid being tortured and then shot as spies, but I did not dwell on this awkward situation for very long because work piled up and it seemed useless to fret about something that might not happen.

THE MEDITERRANEAN

Due to the Shark code having been so difficult to break, there were reasons for growing concern over the Atlantic convoys. As the United States of America had entered the war a year before, the number of ships, both merchantmen and naval escorts, had greatly increased.

It all started on 7th-8th December 1941, a date we shall never forget. On that day the Japanese bombed Pearl Harbour in Oahu, part of the Hawaiian Islands. It was an important and critical U.S. naval base. The Americans were completely taken by surprise and lost nearly all their Pacific Fleet with the exception of two aircraft carriers, which were away on manoeuvres. The intrepid operation by the Japanese came without warning, killing over two thousand American service and civilian personnel, let alone hundreds of wounded. They sank four battleships amongst a total of nineteen warships and one hundred and eighty aircraft. The ease with which this action was performed and made easy for the Japanese was that the American fleet had been assembled in close company in the harbour and the aircraft, for some mysterious reason, were all parked together at one end of the airfield.

It was a disaster incomprehensible to me in retrospect, because American Intelligence together with Bletchley had already broken the Japanese diplomatic code called Magic. They must have been aware that the Japanese Embassy staff in the United States were busy destroying papers and preparing to leave for some time before the raid. Something must have got lost in a tangle of bureaucracy, inducing a sad lack of discrimination and circulation of this paramount cognizance. I can recall at one period that any Ultra material of interest to the United States prior to the arrival at Bletchley of American officers had to be despatched in three envelopes, the middle one marked GUARD in capital letters.

It did seem callous and misplaced to have a sense of euphoria over such a tragedy as Pearl Harbor, but after two years of fighting it alone, it was easy to show our gratitude and difficult not to show our immense relief. It had brought one of the richest countries in the world on our side against Germany. Now the tide must turn, and turn it did, slowly but surely. About a year later Hitler was failing to conquer Russia and he was defeated at Stalingrad. The Russian Army, half-starved and exhausted, counter-attacked with superhuman tenacity and recaptured the outskirts of the city. The German army had overstretched their supply lines and were forced to retreat in bitter weather conditions. The Führer must have forgotten Napoleon!

We did help the Soviets with convoys of munitions and fighter aircraft, and our Army Intelligence huts gave them useful information of German troop movements towards the east and possible attacks on bridgeheads; but only as assessments. The source was never disclosed to them. Churchill did not trust Stalin with what he called his "Golden Eggs".

In November 1942 the Allied Armies landed in north-west Africa. Operation Torch, to give it its code name, became a long-fought campaign to and from Benghazi in Cyrenaica (now Libya) to El Alamein, perilously close to Alexandria in Egypt and too close for comfort to Port Said, the entrance to the Suez Canal. Finally, despite the brilliance of General Rommel and his Afrika Corps, our Eighth Army, under the command of General Montgomery, defeated him at El Alamein.

Rommel had raced his Panzer Divisions twice over that vast expanse of desert, first against our troops under the command of General Wavell followed by General Auchinleck. Nothing seemed to be going right, until along came the jaunty, immeasurably self-confident General Montgomery of the black beret fame — he was under the overall command of General Alexander, who was without doubt one of our finest soldiers. Montgomery was also a good soldier but he had a very special talent. That was his ability to inspire belief and credibility to win into a battle-scarred and war-weary Eighth Army, who as a result surged forward to victory. After all the backward and forward movements, Rommel by this time was running desperately short of fuel due to successful attacks on the German Mediterranean shipping by Allied Air Forces. He was also suffering from ill health and exhaustion and was recalled to Germany.

Even from afar Ultra had a lot to do with this victory, but to begin with there were obstacles to overcome. It proved very difficult to get our sources of information so far afield and yet keep it secure, wireless telegraphy was impossible and landlines equally so. The answer lay in setting up Special Liaison Units amongst the various commands in North Africa to receive Ultra material. These S.L.U.'s, as they were called, consisted of several Special Intelligence officers from Bletchley who were seconded to pass on any knowledge of enemy operations they thought fit.

They were frequently based in uncomfortably small mobile trucks, tents or caravans, access strictly forbidden except to the occupants, where they processed and evaluated Ultra material from B.P. It was their total responsibility to decide, other than the commanding generals, as to who should receive the prodigious material. It must have been an onerous task, often risking the wrath of many a senior officer who wanted to know why a junior in rank in an ill-fitting uniform should be privy to such knowledge and decisions; where had it come from and why should he believe it?

The High Command of course knew from whence it came, as did General Montgomery. We often had more than a sneaking suspicion that he pretended that the decrypts of German positions and their subsequent tactics were his brainchild. After all, it was in his nature that he had to be right. It is not hard to forgive him this little foible for he and his black beret came to be the symbol of faith, courage and endurance of our gallant soldiers.

During this long drawn-out African conflict of bloodshed, thirst and endless sand, I worried terribly about any friends out there. Fortunately, my friend in the army hut came to the rescue. She had found another naval boyfriend by that time and in return for knowledge about his ship, she was able to keep me fairly well informed about our regimental positions. Even to this day I sometimes wake up in a cold sweat at the thought of being found guilty of this minor security lapse and the punishment that would be meted out. I also suffered from an obsession that if I had an accident, I might in anaesthetic coma mumble something about our work. This was coupled with another irrational fear that my undergarments might not be spotless. This trepidation stemmed from the guiding principle of my old nanny, who from early childhood impressed upon me to always wear clean knickers in case I was run over by a bus.

I had an idol in the shape of Admiral Andrew Cunningham, who was Commander-in-Chief Mediterranean. I never met him, alas, but his exploits and sense of humour were legendary in the navy. In March 1941 he knew from Ultra that a large fleet of Italian ships had left Taranto and Brindisi to intercept British convoys. He sailed under darkness from Alexandria in Egypt in his flagship H.M.S. *Warspite* and two other battleships. They despatched three Italian cruisers and two destroyers off Cape Matapan to a watery grave with the loss of one aircraft. This action must have helped future Allied landings in Sicily in 1943 with less enemy shipping to cope with.

Admiral Cunningham was naturally rather pleased with the success of this operation and a signal was promptly sent to Admiralty from C-C. Med stating "I have sunk most of the Italian fleet off Cape Matapan." Some hours went by and he received no reply. This enraged the brilliant, but by now somewhat irascible admiral, who sent another signal to Admiralty which read, "I have been gathering Italians all day, who will you send to take them away?" Perhaps he remembered the nursery rhyme, "Here we come gathering nuts in May."

There were many humorous stories emanating from admirals and senior officers, mainly from Admiral James Somerville who was famous for his badinage, which managed to cheer up his many shipmates. For instance, two destroyers in Malta who were vying for the correct moorage accidentally scraped each other in the bows, which prompted a signal from one of the captains worded "But I've just powdered my nose." Another signal was terse and to the point. Admiral Somerville was taking a naval vessel to the United States for some big conference, when by chance halfway across the Atlantic they met a merchant ship of the same name going the other way. The admiral felt this deserved some kind of recognition and sent a signal saying "Snap."

WORK AND WORRY

I had eight days wonderful leave and was able to visit my parents, but it was hard to get back into the routine; the inability to sleep in the daytime still dogged me, but there was nothing I could do about it except pray for the week to end.

I was working on the Japanese theatre of war at the time, I cannot for the life of me remember why since I could not speak Japanese, except I know that a Maru is a ship. I have a dim memory of doing some analysis on fleet positions, but although I tried to concentrate on the battles, successes or failures of the American fleet, my mind was really in Europe and the Mediterranean. I was thinking of brave little Malta, the George Cross Island who sheltered so many of our ships. The island had been blockaded and suffered horrendous bombing for months and months and its people lived in caves to avoid the downfall of destruction and had not been conquered.

There was a tinge of social life at Bletchley in the form of the Recreation Club where you could play table tennis, known as ping-pong, take part in amateur dramatics, or join a bridge four. Osla and I were too shy at first to apply for membership, but eventually plucked up courage, hoping to be treated to a glass of beer when as applicants we were considered suitable; I am sure everybody was welcome, but we didn't know it at the time. It was in this Recreational Hut, or Beer Hut as it was commonly known, that I was first introduced to alcoholic spirits. It was something called Dutch gin, a pale yellow, oily-looking liquid. I practically burst into flames at the first sip like a volcanic eruption, but as it sank lower into my system my stomach produced a warm glow and I promptly took another swig. The effect of this was instant dizziness and I just about managed to stagger back to my desk.

In the early months of 1943 the atmosphere in the Air Force Hut 3 and Hut 6 was jubilant. It was great news. The 617 Squadron of the R.A.F., flying especially modified Lancaster bombers under the command of Wing Commander Guy Gibson, destroyed the Moehne, Eder and Sorpe dams in the German Ruhr district. This astonishingly brave action was made possible by bouncing bombs. This weapon was the brainchild of a benevolent but prodigious genius called Barnes Wallis. His brief was to design a bomb that could hit the target from aircraft flying as low as 60 feet under cover of darkness, a seemingly impossible task as the dams were heavily defended by anti-aircraft guns and anti-torpedo boom nets. Only a man of Barnes Wallis's calibre would undertake such a crazy assignment and his plan was to make a bomb that would on contact with the water above the dams bounce accurately and explode the walls.

God knows how many hours of practice 617 Squadron must have put in to achieve the impossible and time was short. The dams had to be full and the weather right; but achieve it they did. The bombs were dropped with great accuracy, bouncing and leapfrogging over the upper surface of the water, and breached all three dams. The devastation and flooding caused by this heroic raid must have caused havoc, which of course was the intention. It all but stopped the manufacture of German armaments for hundreds of miles. Sadly, only ten of the nineteen Lancasters came home, but the gallant Guy Gibson won the Victoria Cross for his part as leader.

About the beginning of August 1943, our R.A.F. reconnaissance planes spotted and began to photograph some very strange sights at a place called Peenemunde, north-east of

Lubeck in Germany. They were thin, long, pencil-like objects on the ground facing England. These photographs were sent to the R.A.F. Photo Reconnaissance Unit at Medmenham to be analysed. A particularly brilliant and acute W.A.A.F. officer, after a great deal of magnification, recognised them as rocket launching pads. Agents and other sources had already established that German scientists were working on a self-propelled guided missile; and now the launching territory had been pinpointed. There must have been factories manufacturing these rockets deep underground not too far away, but they could not be detected at the time. On 18th August the R.A.F. bombers inflicted heavy damage on the sites, hopefully delaying production for many months of this solo killer known as the flying bomb, or as the Germans called it, Vergeltungswaffen Nummer Eins. That translated, should have given us a clue that there was a much more unpleasant one to come.

THE *SCHARNHORST* IS DOOMED

There was news in December 1943 that did a lot for the morale of Naval Section and crowned the achievements of Ultra. The Royal Navy had sunk the *Scharnhorst*. After the *Tirpitz* she was, with the *Gneisenau*, one of Germany's finest fighting ships and both to be greatly feared.

I would like at this point to state a personal view with which others may disagree. Admiralty was operational in the sense that all commands to ships, plus tactics and strategy were communicated from within its control, unlike the army and air force, whose orders came from commanders in the field. The story of the savage loss of convoy PQ 17 is typical. Admiralty frequently refused to believe in Ultra and for no good reason in my mind. This curious and somewhat obstructive behaviour continued to puzzle me and probably always will. There are exceptions and the sinking of the *Scharnhorst* is one. The damage she sustained from mines after her Channel dash was eventually repaired and she set sail for Altenfjord to join her sister ship the *Tirpitz*; the latter had been badly damaged by our midget single-manned submarines. They had managed to go through or under her torpedo nets in the fjord and pinned mines against her thick hull, which detonated and made deleterious explosions to her 15-inch armour plating. She was then towed south to Tromsø. Round one to Ultra.

Meanwhile, the *Scharnhorst* had moved to a more remote anchorage from the Norwegian shore. This caused much rejoicing in Naval Section because it meant less use of landlines such as telephones and more of radio signal traffic. By now Bletchley was breaking German naval ciphers with ease.

Perhaps ease is the wrong word, but the flow of signals coming into our office had increased dramatically. Sometimes they came in such bulk that after translation I hardly had time to read them. This might appear to be a baffling contradiction in terms, but we were so used to German signals by that time that we could practically put them into English in our sleep.

On 20th December 1943 a Russian-bound convoy sailed from England. The threat to its safety was of course the *Scharnhorst*. She was the only German seaworthy ship left at that time in those northern waters and she set sail on Christmas Day with the destruction of the convoy as her target. The Commander-in-Chief Home Fleet, Admiral Sir Bruce Fraser in the battleship *Duke of York*, had all the information he needed from Ultra to destroy her. He knew the great battlecruiser had left Altenfjord and, probably due to superb seamanship, where she might be found. Early on 26th December she was attacked by three of our cruisers and lit with star shells on the north coast of Norway. Our guns had blasted away her radar, leaving her navigation blinded. Soon after, she was finished off by the powerful armament from the *Duke of York* and sunk. Round two to Ultra. There now remained the shackled, but ominously lurking *Tirpitz*, but her death blow was to come later.

OPERATION OVERLORD

I was getting tired, restless and a bit stale and for some unknown reason was less interested in my work. It had been eight depressing months with U-boats causing havoc in the Atlantic. Also, I was worried about my brother and my boyfriend, who I believed were both among the Allied troops who had landed on the south-west coast of Italy. My friend in the army hut was not able to give me much information as to their Regiments' positions, although she tried. Eventually I discovered that my brother was with his Regiment, the 5th Battalion, Grenadier Guards at Anzio, north of Naples. The landing was at first unopposed, but the American Allied commander was inexplicably against an immediate advance towards Rome and decided to consolidate in a very small area. This gave the Germans the opportunity to reinforce their defences and as a result the Allied beachhead was in grave danger. I was told the weather was foul and the front line changed constantly. This abortive decision must have been an enormous disappointment to General Alexander, who had wanted to advance and establish a firmer base.

A short while before the Anzio landings and during my malcontented period, I received a flimsy piece of paper in an equally flimsy envelope via the inter-office mail which read as follows:

7.1.44.

Room 121a

Miss Sarah Norton.

As from 1.1.44. you have been promoted to Technical Assistant at 65/- per week.

Signed

A.D. Watson

I was jubilant and completely above the clouds. A rise of ten shillings a week represented a fortune to me and the title of Technical Assistant a worthy prize. Of course we were immediately christened Tech. Asses, which we didn't mind a bit. Osla got elevated too and we celebrated that evening having nicked someone's sweet ration to buy a bar of chocolate.

Little did we know in that moment of exuberance that we would soon be told news of such significance that my breath would be taken away. Our little group from Room 121a and other watches in Naval Section were summoned by our boss, a man called Mac, and told of a momentous event to come. I was a little apprehensive about his request and wondered if I had amongst others done something wrong. I was well aware that I could not be expelled because I knew too much. Once there, no one ever left Bletchley, but there was always a chance that some misdeed would send you back to the dull routine of the Index Room. All these thoughts flitted through my mind as we waited for him to speak, but then I remembered I had just been given a pay rise so the axe was unlikely to fall.

With one of his engaging smiles he asked us to sit down. "You are going to be bigoted," he said. My expression must have been one of total incomprehension, because I knew that a bigot was a person intolerant of any race, religion or creed which hardly applied to us with open minds.

"Don't pay any attention to the meaning of that word. I was not party to the choosing," he said. My face must have registered blank, but he went on to inform us that the Allies were going to invade France in six months' time and he relied on our usual discretion. This extraordinary piece of news was delivered in a flat, matter-of-fact voice and it was a few minutes before we could take in the substance of what we had heard and the utmost secrecy it entailed. Suddenly, as if by the waving of a magic wand, restlessness and ennui vanished. Excitement and exhilaration took its place. The war had taken a new turn which prompted a feverish but hopefully muted frenzy of joy at the thought. From now on every German decrypt would have a broader significance and what they told us would develop into a shaft of light to guide our forces to their ultimate objective.

From January 1944 onwards deception and destruction of the German Air Force had the utmost priority. Plans had been conceived months before. It was imperative before the Allied invasion to liberate France, defeat Germany and protect the landings, that a massive bombing of German airfields and the dislocation of their military system should begin. By night and day clouds of Lancaster bombers and Flying Fortresses darkened the skies, flattening and puncturing Germany's air power. The result of this deadly force, of course, was the slaughter of many civilians, including women and children. Target bombing may be accurate given weak defences, but it also carries away those close to the area. I did not like the thought of killing innocent people any more than anybody else, but nor could I forget the horrors we suffered during the Blitz. It had to be the survival of the fittest, a fact we now had to be thankful for.

Bletchley became even busier than usual, the German Air Force had always relied on their Enigma machines to transmit all orders and information, this had given Hut 3 an invaluable source of knowledge. Decrypts were pouring in with reports of damage done by our planes, giving details of holes on runways, which effectively put the airfields out of action for several days. These were followed by progress reports on repairs and, most important of all, the crippling harm done to the German synthetic oil refineries.

With this reliable information, Bomber Command could react quickly and effectively and as soon as an airfield was repaired another strike of Flying Fortresses zoomed across, dropping their annihilating cargo on the same spot. Heaven only knows what the Germans must have thought about this regular and never-ending continuation of bombing. They could hardly go on blaming the laxity of the Italian intelligence. Perhaps they put it down to increased work by foreign agents working undercover. There was no doubt that by this time Hitler's Germany was being fragmented. The impact and successes of Bomber Command went a long way to achieve and accomplish the Allied landings in Normandy and without Ultra it might not have been possible.

DECEPTION

Deception played an important contribution, almost like Ultra's playmate to the pre-invasion plans, and is a story to fascinate both grown-ups and children as it always has throughout history.

The Germans continued to infiltrate agents into Britain by the usual storybook methods. Some came by parachute, some by sea and landed from submarines. It seemed that due to the brilliant efforts of the intelligence officers of MI5, whose headquarters were in Baker Street, they knew just when and where these spies would arrive and promptly arrested them. If they proved flexible and willing to serve new masters they became double agents and no doubt under strict supervision would radio signals back to Abwehr, the Secret Service of Germany. I imagine at first the misinformation transmitted back to Germany by these recently captured agents was fairly innocuous but interesting enough to gain the confidence of the receiver and after all, Abwehr had every reason to believe the validity of their agents and to trust them. Once this faith had been established it proved easy to lay credence to any ill-informed transmissions.

By this time, what we had long suspected came to pass. Admiral Canaris, Head of the Abwehr, was sacked. Himmler, who controlled military intelligence, which was a division of the S.S. Organisation, hated Admiral Canaris and the feeling was mutual. The admiral was bitterly anti-Nazi and was probably plotting Hitler's downfall. The antipathy was such that we thought he might almost certainly be pro-British, but whatever the truth of the matter, the poor man paid for it with his life and was assassinated.

Naval Section at this time was pretty busy with intercepts from heavy ships of the German Navy based in Norway. Hitler, in his usual deranged process of thought, seemed convinced that we would start an invasion there, despite the perils of landing troops on such rocky and mountainous shores and the dangers of transporting a large force across the turbulent North Sea. Bletchley was happy with his defective concept. He had obviously decided that we would not dare attack across the English Channel. The only alternative in his mind therefore was Norway and he took the bogus fly with all the tenacity of a fresh run salmon. This assembly of Nazi hardware in the wrong place naturally delighted us and geographically it gave us pearls of wisdom. Bletchley's skill in almost instant decryption of the Luftwaffe ciphers made it possible to know whether there were any movement of troops across the Baltic; also the breaking of the Hydra code allowed us further knowledge of any convoy sailings to the north.

There was another great deception about which at first I knew very little, but rumours circulated like tiny zephyrs around our stockade and in Naval Section we pieced them together like a jigsaw.

I think it was Field Marshal von Rundstedt who was convinced that any invasion, other than Norway, would be from the south-east coast of Britain, with a comparatively short and easy passage to the Pas-de-Calais. This is where the ultimate deception came in. The chiefs of staff and Churchill, with prior knowledge from Ultra, ordered a large number of troops to be disposed in the county of Kent. Then came the much-publicised arrival of the American General Patton (somewhat notorious for having slapped wounded soldiers in hospital and accusing them of cowardice) plus some heavily camouflaged tanks and guns made of cardboard. This duplicity must have worked because there were very few German troop movements towards Normandy. This avoided a potentially dangerous situation when our Allied Forces landed on the north-west coast of France.

On 5th April 1944 my week's leave was cancelled and no reason given. A travel ban was imposed, I think it was for all at Bletchley, which lasted until 11th April. I am sure of these dates because the only entry I had to delete from my diary was a dentist appointment on the 8th. At the time I thought "something's up." There were no communications from the outside world except in the utmost emergency. It was like being in a fettered box heavily stamped with sealing wax, but I was soon to know the reason why. The date for Operation Overlord had been chosen. It was hoped to be 6th June, or possibly even during the last hours of 5th June, depending greatly on the weather, which posed a big question mark. We were going to send a vast force of army, navy and air force to invade the shores of Normandy and establish a solid foothold on French soil. From that moment on the U.S. Air Force and Bomber Command deflected their attentions from industrial Germany and concentrated the superior power of their bombers to the railway networks of France and Belgium. Excitement and shivers of anticipation flowed round our perimeter, there was plenty of work to do and we got on with it.

On 12th April I was given forty-eight hours leave and was at last able to contact my mother — we arranged to meet at Claridge's Hotel, where she had booked us a room. I had felt a bit wavery during the train journey, but had no idea that I was dead tired because the adrenalin was still pumping round my veins. My mother took one look at me and said, "Darling, you seem exhausted. What you need is a good meal and a nice glass of vin rosé." That swig of Dutch gin the year before had not in any way prepared me for alcohol mixed with fatigue. I remember enjoying the meal whilst listening to the recent events in her munitions factory and sipping the wine. However, when it came to standing up after dinner, my legs deserted me. Fortunately, I was grabbed by two hovering elderly waiters and had to be half carried to the lifts, barely conscious and quite drunk.

Nobody had ever told me that long hours of concentrated work are not conducive to drinking even half a glass of wine. Upstairs I fell onto the nearest bed, but that proved not to be such a good idea. The pictures had difficulty in staying in one place and the carpet was at sea in a wild storm and I was convinced I had been poisoned. I must have slept a bit that night swearing I would never touch another drop. It was months before I dared go back to Claridge's, certain that my reputation was ruined, but life is about learning and I was learning fast.

Most of May was spent translating urgent intercepts regarding positions of German mines in the English Channel and following the movements of mine-laying ships; albeit routine work it was a vital task to secure the safety of the invasion fleet once it had sailed.

Beyond our blanket of naval security, it was with the greatest relief that we heard that Monte Cassino in Italy had fallen to the Allied Polish troops. It had been a mortally hard slog with many casualties since the earlier landings in Sicily and at Anzio by British and American troops. Both enemy and Allied soldiers had fought with tenacity in foul weather which brought endless rain and subsequent mud. The Poles were superlative troops and, with their hatred of the Germans, were a force to be feared. They fought over this monastery, retreated and fought again until the Polish flag flew proudly over the ruins. The door to Rome was nearly open if not ajar.

THE INVASION OF FRANCE

The code names for all the assault beaches in Normandy had already been chosen and were as follows: Omaha, Utah, Juno, Sword and Gold, but at the beginning of May something very disturbing happened. In an edition of the *Daily Telegraph* newspaper carrying its usual cryptic crossword on the back page were two clues to which the answers were Utah and Omaha.

I cannot recall the clues because I did not see the offending newspaper, but it was noticeable that our heads of sections wore deeply worried frowns with choleric complexions, and our mathematical geniuses looked as if they had suffered a direct hit from a high-explosive bomb. Undoubtedly they must have been some of the first to spot the possibility of our invasion plans being leaked, because whatever shift or watch they were on, a tea break usually inspired a race as to who could complete any crossword in the shortest possible time. Time meaning whether it was quicker to go straight through the across clues followed by the down ones or fill them in as they went along, I don't think the answers were ever any problem. The potential disaster of Ultra falling into enemy hands was thankfully averted when it was discovered quite soon that the setter of the crossword had used Utah and Omaha in all innocence and that it was just an unfortunate coincidence.

In the second week of May, General Eisenhower, Commander-in-Chief of all Allied Forces, decided the date for D-Day was to be 6th June for the invasion of Europe. The smug occupants of Room 121a in Hut 4, Naval Section were informed of this — we considered it our right to know, which in retrospect was pretty saucy considering our bumptiousness had been given a nasty knockback during the autumn of 1943. The Germans had invented an acoustic torpedo for submarines, I think we developed one about the same time, but this wonder weapon gave Admiral Dönitz of U-Boat Command the extra fervour he needed to attack our convoys once more. It had not been so easy for him at that time. Bletchley was decrypting current traffic almost continuously, we had many more surface escort vessels for each convoy coupled with Liberator aircraft, which had a range of eight hundred miles. This virtually closed the mid-Atlantic gap, which had haunted us for nearly four years, and they were able to give the voyage of any convoy uninterrupted cover. However, this nasty sound-seeking weapon could do a lot of damage and something had to be done to offset its effectiveness.

For some bizarre reason, I and the other occupants of Room 121a decided to put our collective brains together to work out a device to waylay or destroy this torpedo. I don't know what possessed us to think of ourselves as boffins or even presume to be embryo scientists, but we were too busy with progressive thoughts to worry about this.

The answer came relatively quickly and seemed totally obvious, a long cable could be attached to the stern of each ship at the end of which would be towed a loud motor engine, this engine would attract the acoustic mechanism of the torpedo and save the ship. The joint thesis was proudly presented to the head of Naval Section, who decently skimmed over the contents with a beatific smile and told us Admiralty had already thought of that and it was working out quite nicely. He did, however, compliment us on our initiative, but deflated our overindulged egos by suggesting that we got back to the job we were paid to do.

At the beginning of June 1944 electronics came to Bletchley. I was totally out of my depth there, but with various discreet questions from my esoteric sources, I gathered that our present Bombes were electromagnetic and that Professor Alan Turing, along with the electronic wizard T. E. Flowers of the Post Office Research Station at Dollis Hill, were working together desperately anxious to speed up the process of decipherment. Tommy Flowers decided to employ 1,500 thermionic valves instead of the electromagnetic relays. These apparently propelled the undertaking into the world of electronics and thus Colossus was born. The speed of decryption of this machine was remarkable and Colossus began operating at B.P. in February 1944, followed by Mark II using 2,400 valves. By the end of the war ten Colossi were in service at Bletchley. I am still bemused and confounded but thank God for Tommy Flowers and Alan Turing.

D-Day, 6th June, was approaching rapidly and we worked non-stop and worried about the weather. The meteorological reports were not good for that day — rain and storms would be devastating to our forces. Despite this alarming scenario, the powers that be decided to go ahead with their plans, so all we could do now was to work and pray.

On 5th June I was given, to my surprise, forty-eight hours leave and it was with much relief that I disencumbered myself of the piles of signals, waved goodbye to my cronies and caught the first train to London. My two days of leisure were unexpected and I was unsure as to where to stay. Luckily my aunt, who worked with gliders, was at home in her house in Chester Row, Belgravia. She was always welcoming and would never refuse to give a bed or even a sofa to me and many of my friends who turned up at the last minute. She also did a magnificent job as an unpaid receptionist in the shape of receiving messages and telephone calls from those who turned up on leave. Keeping in touch was hard enough in wartime, but from Bletchley it was virtually impossible. Unfortunately, my aunt was on duty that evening and I dreaded being alone on such a momentous night. I could not have told her the reason for my fear and fretfulness and had looked forward to her company, sharing the usual meal of dried eggs and canned fruit. It was therefore with great pleasure that she told me a heavily pregnant friend of mine tucked away out of danger in the country had left a message to the effect that her husband was free for dinner, and would I meet him at The Berkeley Hotel in Piccadilly at 8.30 p.m.

I ran the bathroom taps up to the regulation three inches, put on a rather nasty utility red crepe dress and was disgusted to find my only lipstick was orange, causing my complexion to be even pastier than usual; no time for reflective gloom, however, so I ran to Sloane Square to find a bus. The driver, bless him, called me darling and dropped me off at The Ritz, opposite my destination. As I got off the bus the sky looked ominous, black and heavy with cloud, the air was damp and discouraging and the rain was minutes away. I was fortunate that all I had to do was to cross the road and try to quench my unease.

My friend's husband was very good-looking and great fun to be with. He had a pretty high up job in the Foreign Office and was distinguished in many fields of Foreign Affairs. The food was as good as it could be under rationing and I tried to keep my concentration on his charming company instead of our invasion force. I found it sometimes quite astonishing that during the war one was able to enjoy conversations with

136

people without ever mentioning the jobs that we were doing — I do not know how on earth we managed it. All we had to speak about were relations and the latest news from the daily newspapers, all of them heavily censored by the Ministry of Propaganda, the difficulties of food rationing and other related subjects. I was egotistic enough to realise that I knew more secrets than most people, but equally aware that the information could not be divulged for at least thirty years.

After dinner, at about 11.30 p.m., we stood outside the hotel with one umbrella between us waiting for a possibly non-existent taxi. The rain by then was coming down in sheets, almost obliterating the indistinct blur of the street lights, and a forbidding blackness surrounded us. Suddenly I heard a sound that I had been expecting, at first a distant hum and then a low murmuring with monotonous intensity. It got louder and more resonant and my eardrums started to pound when suddenly the sky, already dark with rain, was made even darker by the sight of R.A.F. bombers towing gliders over London, covering the city with a mighty shroud. There were 1,136 planes bound for the shores of Normandy and my heart went with them as they flew.

My friend, who as far as I knew was not privy to Ultra, was rendered almost speechless by this overpowering vision and he asked me if I knew what was going on. I replied I hadn't the faintest idea and hoped my voice sounded steady enough. It must have been sheer ingrained habit to keep the knowledge secret, because by the next morning the British public was informed that the invasion had begun.

At 11.55 that evening, 5th June, Major John Howard led his men, part of the 6th British Airborne Division, and they landed their gliders at a place called Benouville, near the Caen canal bridge in Normandy. which was in the area of the Sword beachhead. The ground was very marshy but the landings succeeded with six gliders to capture all the vital bridges. One of the bridges is particularly memorable and christened Pegasus. I don't know why, except that it seemed a suitable pseudonym bearing in mind the mythical flying horse. In retrospect it lives in the minds of those brave paratroopers who, having captured this bridge and marched across, were astonished to be greeted by two young French ladies who owned a tiny house, more of a kiosk really, called Café Gondrée. They were immensely hospitable, offering cups of tea and coffee, which must have been a lovely surprise for the men of the Airborne Division.

Early in the morning of Tuesday 6th June, I thought I had better get back to work. Despite being on leave I really wanted to know what was going on, so I caught the milk train to Bletchley. On arrival in Hut 4 the air was jubilant and even reclusive souls were happy to give away little titbits. I discovered that it wasn't until 1.30 a.m. on the 6th that the German Army realised that our troops had made a landing, but General von Rundstedt thought it was a deception to cover the real invasion at Calais. At about 5 a.m. the news reached Berchtesgaden, Hitler's retreat in the mountains, but apparently no one dared wake him from his usual drugged sleep and he was not informed until 9 a.m.

Later that day, after I had gone off duty, Bletchley produced decrypts showing that the Germans expected further landings other than Normandy, but had no idea where they would be. Once again this proved that the great deception that we would attack the Pas-de-Calais had been swallowed hook, line and sinker. The result of this duplicity was that not only the 116 Panzer Division, but almost the entire German Army was floundering about not knowing whether to march east or west.

It might have been funny if the consequences had not been so serious. To quote Ronald Lewin in his brilliant book *Ultra Goes to War*, "it was a triumph which in retrospect scarcely seems possible without Ultra."

Our naval assault force was called Operation Neptune. After considerable pounding by our warships onto the Normandy shores together with gallant activity by the French Resistance, the attack on the beaches began. Neptune sent out 1,213 ships from battleships to midget submarines, there were also 4,000 landing craft and other small boats. It must have been the largest invasion fleet that ever sailed. Our minesweepers had done a wonderful job clearing the Channel of mines and a great tribute to them was that only one Allied destroyer was sunk by those sinister black globes with rounded antenna. This vast armada of ships had set off from as far west as Plymouth and Newhaven to the east, sailing for the designated beaches.

The Germans still remained convinced that there would be other landings and they stuck firmly to their idea that our objective was the Pas-de-Calais. The Double-Cross System continued to be effective with captured enemy spies having been "TURNED" to broadcast what we instructed them to do. The R.A.F. compounded this deception by flying over Boulogne and Calais, dropping slivers of tinfoil to baffle the German radar into thinking that the invasion fleet was headed in that direction.

Other snippets of information were delightful. The commander of the 21st Panzer Division was not about on the morning of D-Day and was reputed to be with his French mistress, but he was not the only person absent. General Rommel had attended his wife's birthday party and did not return to his base until the afternoon. General von Rundstedt, C in C. West, appeared totally unimpressed when he received the news that the German radar was being jammed with special messages to the French Resistance between Cherbourg and Le Havre. (I can only presume that his conviction that our landings had to be in the Pas-de-Calais had convoluted his mind to such an extent that no esoteric information or influence would change it.) In hindsight it does seem strange that such an undoubtedly brilliant General could show such insularity.

At about 5 p.m. on the evening of 6th June, Hitler sent out orders that the beachhead must be eliminated at once. What he did not appear to realise, though, was that there was not one beachhead but five. That signal must have given great pleasure to those in Hut 6 at Bletchley.

DOODLEBUGS

My memory fails me as to what happened during the next few weeks, mainly I think because there was so much work to do. Decrypts were pouring in like monsoon rain and excitement nearly superseded my concentration. According to my diaries, if you can dignify them by that name, there was nothing at all. They would have been pretty poor reading anyway, just a dentist appointment for the future or letter from a friend, but on 13th June I had written "four days leave after day watch." Funnily enough, it was the first time in my years at Bletchley that I didn't want even temporarily to leave my work. All part of wanting to be in the centre of the action, I suppose.

I caught the first train somewhat reluctantly to Euston, it was as usual jam-packed with service personnel, no chance of a seat and no chance of falling over. I was wedged firmly between two burly soldiers who offered me a Woodbine cigarette. I thought smoking was awfully sophisticated but had to refuse because I couldn't move my arms.

I had decided to spend a few days with my mother. She was still slogging away in her armaments factory and getting very tired, she was only forty-four, but never having done a day's work in her life before the war, was finding it increasingly exhausting and I was worried about her. It was whilst I was staying with her in Surrey that a nasty new weapon of destruction came our way. Hitler called these self-propelled rockets Vergeltungswaffen No. 1 and 2. *Vergeltung* in German means retaliation or reprisal and a very nasty counter-stroke they were too.

On 15th June 1944, I awoke in leafy Surrey to a strange noise, no insistent drumming of Dornier and Heinkel bombers, but a more tinny sound advancing near ground level. I jumped out of bed and ran into the garden fearful that perhaps one of our aircraft was in trouble, and an astounding sight presented itself in the shape of a small glider, but with a tiny propeller at the pointed front and fire blazing out of its tail. It flew over the cottage at about 500 feet towards London and out of sight, but I could still hear its engine until it suddenly stopped and after a few seconds I heard a massive explosion.

The penny dropped. It was one of those rocket machines from the launchpads that Air Reconnaissance had previously photographed at Peenemünde in the Baltic. These doodlebugs, as they came to be known, were intended to fall on central London, but fortunately many of them were shot down by the R.A.F. in the Channel and a good few were purposely misdirected by the efforts of double agents, who reported back to Germany that strikes were landing beyond the city. This forced the enemy to cut down the range and save London. There were thousands of these lethal buzz bombs aimed at us, most of which detonated on the unfortunate inhabitants of Kent and Essex who bravely bore the brunt.

After a few days of unremitting attack by these unpleasant aerial torpedoes, the people of southern England discovered that they were safe until the engine cut out. You then counted to fifteen and dived for whatever cover was available because at that point the flying bomb exploded. The warhead carried almost a ton of explosives, causing damage in a large radius. It shattered windows, causing splinters of glass to fly in all directions and severely wounding anyone standing up, while roof tiles and debris shot into the air, falling indiscriminately on the wretched victims. This secret weapon was meant to demoralise us, but like others it failed. We had taken worse and remained as stoical as ever.

On my next visit to my mother I was able to vent my fury on these fiendish machines in a seemingly imbecilic way, but it wasn't quite as stupid as it sounds. Behind my mother's cottage there was a large dense wood, quite a few acres in dimension and mostly comprised of ancient yew forest. The flying bombs were now coming in very low, barely skimming the treetops and at an alarming speed, which indicated an immediate cut of the engine before plummeting to earth. Rage filled my entire body and without thinking I picked up an old brick and hurled it at the thing. To my astonishment I scored a hit, the engine coughed, spluttered, limped on and exploded further on into the thick wood. I was extremely pleased with myself for saving some of the population and houses beyond. I never managed to hit another, but not for want of trying. My aim had always been useless, hopeless at bowling for cricket and although I played tennis in exquisite style, I hardly ever came into contact with the ball, I hit more divots on the golf course than it was possible to believe and at the age of seven made a bonfire of my specially made golf clubs in a tantrum.

My mother, who detected that I was a little too puffed up with pride at the direct hit, suggested with a touch of sarcasm that whatever I was doing now I would be more use joining an anti-aircraft battery since I was so good at hitting things. Later that evening I began to realise that a garden brick could not have possibly deflected the flying bomb. My action was just a reflection of the anger I felt at the time, but as I fell asleep I thought, perhaps it did?

On my way back to Bletchley I heard some despairing news, one of the V1 robots had fallen on the Guards' Chapel at

Wellington Barracks, killing over a hundred people. It completely destroyed the beautiful building and apart from one girl in the A.T.S. who realised what the cut-out meant and ran out of the door, the congregation were all left in the chapel. A few days later a V1 destroyed the tennis court at Buckingham Palace. If only Ultra could find the underground bunkers where these weapons were stored — they were certainly not close to the launching pads. There was no doubt that we would find them, but when?

At Bletchley, like the rest of the British public, our spirits see-sawed, one day weary, the next day elated by some good piece of news. We were sick with anxiety over the battle for Caen where a Panzer Division had dug itself in, obstinately refusing to be removed, regardless of losing most of its officers and facing hundreds of 16-inch shells fired with precision from the battleship H.M.S. *Rodney*.

In Naval Section we were, I think, less worried and frenetic about our precious navy because, due to Ultra together with unsurpassed seamanship, most enemy surface vessels were prevented to a large extent from interfering with the Allied invasion. The reason for this fortunate situation was that we had sunk the *Scharnhorst*. The *Tirpitz* was skulking in a Norwegian fjord, the R.A.F. had badly lacerated the *Gneisenau* and the *Hipper*, putting them temporarily out of action, and the pocket battleships *Scheer* and *Lutzow* were refitting or perhaps even supporting the German Army in the Baltic. With these horrific giants out of the way, the Channel was only fortified with a few enemy destroyers and a flotilla of speedy E-boats. These ships, of course, were being constantly strafed by the dominance of our air force.

BOMB PLOT AND PARIS LIBERATED

Everything eventually filtered through to Bletchley. The most exciting at the time was the plot to kill Hitler and it was doomed to failure. We had always assumed that any effort to get rid of this monster could only be achieved by his enemies inside Germany, whoever they were. The poor tortured Jews emaciated and starving in the brutal labour camps could do nothing but try to stay alive, and very few of them managed this.

There was a strong resistance movement within Germany like the Maquis in France, but they were hampered by lack of organisation and weaponry, unlike the French who benefited from R.A.F. Lysanders who were able to drop agents, explosives, rifles and ammunition into their unoccupied territory. I was told, but cannot verify it, that although Churchill knew of this German secret activity, he categorically refused to have anything to do with them. Whether he was right or wrong is anybody's guess, but it would have been impossible to supply them with sufficient arms. The assassination plot therefore came from those much closer to him and it failed by a whisker.

Colonel von Stauffenberg, an aristocrat and a patriot, together with his fellow plotters devised a plan to kill Hitler by placing a bomb in a briefcase as near as possible to him during a meeting at Rastenberg in East Prussia. Von Stauffenberg attended the conference and placed the briefcase under the table as near to Hitler as possible, he then made an excuse to leave the H.Q.

Unfortunately, one of the other generals present moved the briefcase back in order to get a closer look at the large-scale map on the table. Within seconds there was a loud explosion, sending bodies flying through the windows. Hitler's eardrums were punctured, his arm slightly paralysed and he had burns on his legs. A mischance had saved his evil life. Meanwhile, von Stauffenberg, hearing the explosion and certain that Hitler had been killed, hurried off to catch a plane to Berlin and report his successful mission to his anti-Nazi colleagues.

Curiously enough, Hitler, despite his wounds, the other casualties and the debris caused by the bomb, saw fit to receive a visit from Mussolini, who had himself just escaped an assassination plot in Italy. It seemed a very inappropriate moment to do so. Perhaps they wanted to exchange personal particulars of their salvation as well as tactics. At this point the dreaded Himmler stepped in. One of the generals at the meeting who had not been injured during the blast had noticed the swift and surprising departure of von Stauffenberg and sounded the alarm. At once a nationwide hunt began for anti-Nazi plotters and several thousand men and women, some innocent, were sent to the Gestapo torture cells. The wretched von Stauffenberg was captured immediately, taken into the courtyard of the War Ministry and shot. Perhaps he was lucky. Instant death was infinitely preferable to the torture by Himmler's roughnecks who were skilled in persecution.

Occasionally a piece of delectable news came our way, not necessarily to do with Naval Intelligence and sometimes it was not very important, but it did give us great pleasure. In this case it concerned the Royal Air Force — a Gloster Meteor jet from 616 Squadron came across a V1 doodlebug somewhere over the English Channel. The pilot fired to destroy it but his guns jammed, so with the utmost presence of mind he caught up with the missile and tipped it over by inserting his wing tip under the rocket's wing and sent it hurtling out of control earthward, or probably seaward. The pilot saved a few lives and gave great satisfaction to the inmates of Room 121a by his contribution to enemy destruction.

Another enormous bestowal to our war effort and a blessing to the Allied Armies in France was the invention of PLUTO, the acronym for Pipe-Line Under The Ocean. This pipeline kept fuel flowing uninterrupted across the Channel to supply the troops who were at last advancing in Normandy. I don't think the Germans ever found out about this liquid gold cable and I wondered why it did not seem strange to them that we were never short of fuel, as they often were.

In the middle of August more good news. The American Seventh Army landed on the beaches of the French Riviera. They secured a foothold between Cannes and St Tropez with the help of the French Resistance, who were very strong in the area. I don't think there were any collaborators amongst those brave southern French citizens. The occupying Germans would throw half-smoked cigarettes into the gutters and the French would spit on them even though they were longing for a puff.

On that same day, 15th August, the Paris police went on strike. They kept their arms and joined the Resistance. In retaliation the Germans cut off the city gas supply. We hoped that the cooking facilities were as difficult for them as for the Parisians, who were half-starved as it was.

Another day of rejoicing on 24th August was the reopening of the London theatres, which had been closed during the V1 flying bomb offensive. Those of us owed some leave dashed up to London and met at the Shaftesbury Theatre. I cannot remember what the play was about, which was a pity because it was quite an occasion to sit in a public place without fear of reprisal from overhead.

The next day was crowned by Paris being liberated. General von Choltitz, the commander of that area, surrendered to the French 2nd Armoured Division under General Leclerc. It was very fitting that the Free French should be the first to enter their own capital city. There were still some active German snipers around but that did not stop the townspeople, who were nearly hysterical with joy, from cheering as the troops marched down the Champs Elysees from the Arc de Triomphe. The fight for the liberation of Paris, however, was not quite over. The snipers had to be mopped up, which resulted in a lot of innocent people being shot. The collaborators too were rounded up. I hate to think what happened to them, all those years of victimisation; threats and semi-starvation were not conducive to kind treatment towards traitors.

To celebrate the deliverance of this great French city, Osla and I decided to give a party in the Beer Hut. We had been at Bletchley long enough to get to know people outside Naval Section, which made quite a merry gathering. Service personnel from our Hut 4 were forbidden entrance unless they were in uniform, the lure of the gold braid still dazzled us. Drink was a bit of a problem, yet Osla managed to purloin two bottles of Dutch gin and refused to divulge where they came from. My mother sent me by the usual P.O. address three packets of soggy biscuits that she had stolen from her factory canteen. I used up my months' sweet ration to supply chocolates together with some disgusting Liquorice Allsorts and the weak beer was obtainable from the linoleum-covered bar. It was quite a jolly evening with people drifting in and out from various watches, and we got sociable with gentlemen we had previously been in awe of and found them quite human, even jovial.

The naval officers flirted with us but not, unfortunately, in a serious way, except for one under the influence of drink who swore eternal allegiance to Osla. The party had an amazing effect; by the next day the population of this diverse compound began to recognise us. They smiled, waved and generally treated us in a compatible way. Whether the load of secrecy and security had led us all into small select groups we will never know, but for Osla and me the general atmosphere at Bletchley had lightened together with our more successful war efforts.

Some events in the sea warfare, however, were not so good. Admiral Dönitz had managed to build up his U-boat fleet in the Atlantic and was again threatening our convoys. His acoustic torpedo, known disdainfully to Naval Intelligence as "Gnat", was his pride and joy, but mercifully it did not always hit the target; frequently the torpedo exploded on encountering the wake of a ship or the buffeting of the heavy Atlantic seas. Intercepts revealed two emergency signals from U-boats reporting having been torpedoed and sinking. This could only mean that they had been attacked by their own "Gnats" due to poor visibility or malfunction. This limitation prompted Dönitz to order them to be used only in good weather. The deputy director of Naval Intelligence with his usual wisdom decided to let the Germans think their prize weapon was successful in all its missions and have them presume our shipping losses were correct in their estimates instead of advising them of the vagaries of the torpedo. With the enemy's uncertainty as to where the actual Allied invasion was likely to be, U-Boat Command was placed in a predicament as to where to place their submarines and as a result they were diversified in such areas as the Baltic, the northern Bay of Biscay and further south in case we attempted to land near Bordeaux. This was highly satisfactory because Dönitz still had about 400 U-boats operational and their dispersal was a great help to us, it was an enormous tribute to the cryptographers at B.P. for breaking the devilish Shark submarine code which told us where they were lurking.

V.E. ROCKETS

Early in September 1944 we, the British public, were told that the danger of flying bombs was practically over. There were sighs of relief all round and also the blackout had been partially lifted, but we were still required to draw the curtains during any possible raid. It was called a "dim-out" which gave us a chance to chuck away the hideous black bombazine-type material which lined them. Up until now woe betide anyone who showed the merest chink of light. If you were careless enough to do so the air-raid wardens would be down on you like a ton of bricks and a stern warning issued. The shadow of death and peril was still to come in the shape of the terrifying V2 rockets. I had been frightened before during the past four years on occasions when bombs whistled close by, but they became a fact of life and something that had to be borne as stoically as possible with the minimum of fuss. There were those philosophical types who held the theory that a bomb had their name on it. This ideology seemed to release them from any obligation to take cover, much to the annoyance of the yellow-helmeted wardens whose job it was to rescue people. I did not subscribe to this concept entirely and always tried to take evasive action, even under a kitchen table, whenever possible.

The exception to this rule of semi-safety happened once during the Blitz in Berkeley Square. My mother had bought me a new winter coat, it was bottle-green with a fur collar, I thought it terribly smart and felt like a model out of *Vogue* magazine as I enjoyed the admiring glances from passers-by on my way to the Ritz Hotel. Suddenly the air-raid sirens blasted off, but as I was late for my appointment I paid no attention and went on my way. A moment later a big high-explosive bomb fell at the bottom of St. James's Street which nearly destroyed the palace, the blast from it snaked its path up to Piccadilly and blew round the corner into Berkeley Square. The force of it was considerable, but despite the drizzling rain I managed to keep on my feet, only to be thrown into the gutter by some overzealous warden. I knew he had my safety at heart, but my beautiful coat was covered with slimy muck. I am ashamed to say I lost my temper and screamed like a banshee at the poor man, "Look what you have done to my new coat." Vanity had completely dispersed fear in those few minutes and I arrived at the Ritz looking like a mangled sewer rat.

I didn't experience the V2 rockets at first, being resident at Bletchley, but the baptism of fire was not far away. What was particularly unnerving was that you could not hear them coming, the sirens were useless so no warning of impending doom, they just descended from the sky unannounced, forming a huge crater, killing people and destroying buildings in a large area. The enemy had new launch sites in Holland and as most of the mechanics who serviced the rockets lived somewhere else underground, all they had to do was to transport them to the launch sites, fuel them and ignite. The crew then evacuated the site, leaving only a small pencil-like target for our aircraft to destroy, a near impossible task.

This was indubitably the nastiest weapon London and the south-east had to suffer. There was no chance of stopping them as their velocity was 3,600 miles per hour, the explosive warhead weighed one ton and carried a mixture of T.N.T. and ammonium nitrate. It flew at about 10,000 feet and its horizontal range was two hundred miles. What could we do but accept the demolition of our countryside and its people and pray that our armies would eventually reach the sites and destroy them?

In the microcosm of Naval Intelligence the great battleship *Tirpitz* was always in the foreground of our consciousness. Would she leave the comparative safety of Altenfjord and threaten our shipping? She was well capable of causing immense damage. Or would she lie dormant like a stowaway? One of our intelligence analysts told me he thought Hitler was afraid she might be damaged and would not risk her going to sea, but the problem continued to exercise the mighty brains at Bletchley and O.I.C. as to how to get rid of this menace.

Bomber Command very nearly succeeded in her elimination, about the middle of September. On 15th September 1944 two squadrons of Lancasters were sent to a place in northern Russia which was within their range of Altenfjord. In their attempt to dispose of the *Tirpitz*, despite fighter defences and smokescreens, they managed to secure one hit and two misses. This hit was unknown at the time to the squadrons because, due to bad visibility from the smoke pots, it must have seemed sensible to get out while the going was good. Ultra confirmed four days later from a decrypt to all German military attachés that a bomb had hit the ship's fo'c'sle at the bow end, where the crew and stores are quartered, and had peeled back the deck like a broken blister. Repairs could not be done on the spot. As a result the *Tirpitz* was moved south to Tromsø. Fortunately, she was now within range of operations in this country and would have to await her doom.

Rumour began to circulate that Hitler was going mad. It occurred to me that he had been psychotic from the start and could not be any madder. Nevertheless it was with considerable pleasure to learn from unidentified sources of his fits of temper and deep depressions. I was happy to think of him hiding away in his underground bunker at Rastenberg with bloodshot eyes and trembling hands pondering about his overstretched resources scattered across Europe and the Baltic states. For the defence of Germany he had to call upon raw recruits who knew little of fighting; also he did not seem to heed the advice of his professional generals and relied solely on the heads of the Nazi Party.

The consequence of this disorientated thinking was to be the death of his finest soldier, Field Marshal Rommel. On 14th October 1944 Rommel was visited at his home near Ulm by two Nazi henchmen. Perhaps this is not so surprising as his name had been linked to the July plot to assassinate Hitler. We do not know what was said during that interview, but afterwards Rommel went upstairs to see his wife. When he came down he told his son Manfred that he would be dead within a quarter of an hour. He took poison almost immediately to save his family from being arrested, the official communiqué was that he had died of wounds received from the strafing of his staff car in North Africa and was given a state funeral. Oddly enough I think most of our military personnel felt a pang of remorse at the untimely death of a brave and resolute soldier who had done nothing wrong other than to fight gallantly for his country.

A NEW JOB

On 18th October 1944 I had a summons from my boss, the head of Naval Section. I wasn't too worried this time as any minor misdemeanour which I may have perpetrated had either been missed or overlooked, he seemed his usual chirpy self and invited me to take a seat.

"Now," he said, "I've got a new job for you." I felt a certain frisson of fear and the quickening of my pulses at this statement. I was certainly not a candidate for the Z Room, their capabilities were far beyond my mental level, and I wondered what on earth was coming. He continued by telling me details of the changes he proposed for me in a voice tinged with amusement. "You are aware," he said, "that in the past we have experienced difficulties with Admiralty or rather the admirals in getting them to accept material assessed from Ultra with no questions asked." I replied that I was and had heard rumours to that effect.

"Well," he said, "I think we have solved that problem. Commander Bacon has suggested that we set up an office within the confines of Operational Intelligence Centre at Admiralty." I must have looked distracted enough for him to pause. After a moment or two he said, "Don't look so worried and startled, I am sending you up there to join three other girls from this section and your office will be called N.I.D. 12A."

In a more quizzical tone he went on to tell me, "We need increased co-operation from the high-ups and the admirals, so it will not be a bad thing to smile prettily at the gold-braided gentlemen when you visit them for the information we need, such as departures and arrivals of fleet vessels and merchant convoys. Effectively you girls will be liaison officers between Bletchley and Admiralty." I didn't know whether my face expressed amazement or amusement, but I managed to blurt out, "Sir, are you giving me this job for my brains or for my exceptionally good legs?" To which he replied, "A bit of both will come in handy. You will report for duty on November 3rd and be briefed when you get there."

In true Bletchley fashion nothing more was said and I drifted back to Room 121a in a daze. My peers were kind enough to congratulate me, not so much for the promotion, if indeed it was one, but for the luck and enchantment of getting up to London and they hoped I would be able to avoid the V2s.

It was a good excuse to give a farewell party in the Beer Hut. Drink by then was not so difficult to obtain, but still restricted to weak lager and that wicked Dutch gin which now tasted like alcoholic cough mixture. Many toasts were drunk, I cannot particularly remember who to and certainly not all directed towards me, the party just seemed a good reason to raise our glasses in convivial hilarity.

As I was due to depart Bletchley on 1st November, I felt I should inform my parents that I was leaving wherever they thought I was and moving up to London to work at the Admiralty. This presented a problem as to where I should live. I could not impose on my aunt for too long, she had her own family back from America to house and therefore I had nowhere to go.

This lack of home base in London didn't seem to have bothered me at the time. I was too excited about my new job, and although I had a certain affection for Bletchley Park, plus all my friends I had made over the years, I had been feeling a little stale and restless. I needed a challenge and this was it.

My mother soon had my living accommodation sorted out
— a great-uncle of mine who lived in Cheshire owned a flat in
Arlington Street off Piccadilly close to the Ritz Hotel. He was
quite content for me to live there, it was a prime location and it
would only take me a short time to walk to work. My mother
gently pointed out that to use the Ritz as a watering hole would
not be a good idea because I couldn't afford it; also it would be
a mistake to buy groceries at Fortnum and Mason. Instead I
should find a small corner shop and when off duty it would be
advisable to learn to cook.

My upbringing had been utopian, centred round a large
country house in Scotland with a large staff. My brother and I
loved them dearly and I think they must have spoilt us a lot.
The result was I was sorely unprepared to do anything for
myself, although I had learned by then to wash my underwear
with strict instructions from Nanny to use plenty of soap
flakes, Lux if obtainable. Nanny, whom we adored, was very
insistent on good manners, naughty behaviour at the tea table
was not to be countenanced and would draw a swift rebuke
such as "We did not ask Mr. Rude to tea." Questions like
"Nanny, where are we going?" drew the reply, "There and back
to see how far it is and don't scuff your new shoes," whilst in
response to "Nanny, how old are you?" she would smile and
say, "I am as old as my tongue and a little older than my teeth."
It was an idyllic childhood and even then I knew I was lucky.

ARRIVAL IN LONDON

On 3rd November I left Bletchley never to return. It was a painful departure in numerous ways and many tears were shed in Naval Section, mostly by me. I somehow wanted to recapture the strange atmosphere of the place before it flew away. I had grumbled enough about the restrictions and the limitations of our life there, but there was a certain magic about the place and what the people in it had achieved without the benefit of killing machines. I had become part of it and now was loth to leave. There was one consolation, however; B.P. had a direct line to O.I.C. Admiralty and therefore the communications between friends would be constant.

The next morning Osla went mournfully off to work, just managing as usual to catch the transport at the end of the drive. I said farewell and a thousand thanks to our dear landlords and providers of comfort and got into a taxi with the same battered cardboard suitcase, by this time tied with rope, but minus our gramophone and records, which I thought would remind Osla of our happy times together in the attic.

On arrival in London I had to get another taxi, this was getting expensive. I must have looked pretty bedraggled on reaching Arlington House because the porter gave me the keys to the flat rather reluctantly and eyed my luggage with a rheumy sniff. The flat was a dream come true. It had a bedroom with a double bed, a bathroom, kitchen and a big sitting room facing south-west towards St James's Palace, definitely "Port Out Starboard Home" compared to what I had been used to. The furniture was old, a bit tattered and to my astonishment the walls were hung with some very fine oil paintings. I couldn't think what possessed my great-uncle to leave them there in wartime, but he was very absent-minded, a bachelor, a bit batty and had probably forgotten they were there. He was also God's gift to children, because he did everything upside down and inside out. When you arrived to stay with him he would embrace you fondly and ask you to visit him again soon and when you were leaving he would tell you how happy he was that you had come. He had a dressing-up trunk for us to pretend to act plays. I was particularly fond of wearing a necklace of gold-coloured beads, but someone in the family took them to the British Museum who confirmed that they were 400 B.C. Naturally I never saw them again.

Whilst musing about my delightful old relative, my eyes caught sight of a telephone. It was an early model shaped like a demented daffodil which acted as the mouthpiece with a listening handle hanging by a hook and a dialling circle at the base. You could do wicked things with these instruments such as putting the handle to the mouthpiece, which hit the person ringing with a devilish screech that nearly pierced their eardrums. It was a useful way to get rid of unwanted callers. I hoped it was still working and picked up the handle to hear the welcoming burr. Eureka! I was in touch with the world.

Next on the schedule was food. Piccadilly was not noted for its friendly village grocer and I was forced to provision myself from one of the elite emporia, confining myself to a loaf of bread, milk and hard cheese. The first night was pretty lonely. I had been used to the company of my peers for four years and most people I knew in London were either away or on nightshift. I tried to think about my new job, which was a fairly useless occupation since I did not know what it entailed. Then came the crashing and unwanted welcome of a V2 rocket nearby. I had always felt reasonably confident under fire, amongst others you could either talk or gabble and pretend it wasn't happening, but all alone five storeys up was a different matter. I decided to venture down to the ground floor for some human support. I found humans alright, in fact the entire hall space was covered with them. I found a corner to sit down and engaged one or two in conversation. They had very funny accents and strange uniforms, and for one deranged second I thought they looked and spoke like Germans.

The ancient porter, who by that time had developed the father and mother of a streaming cold, told me they were the Free Dutch who had taken over most of the building during hostilities. I found this very interesting and decided to enliven the rather morbid atmosphere by telling a few of my jokes which always went down well during bombing raids, but my attempts to create some amusement were a dismal failure. Not one smile creased their wary faces and it was evident that despite their bravery, a sense of humour was not their forte. This was all rather depressing, so I went back up to my flat and had a little cry in solitary confinement. Fortunately, great-uncle had left behind — along with his precious paintings — a good selection of beautifully bound Victorian novels. The first one I picked out was called *The Boxer Rebellion* by Captain F. S. Brereton. Both title and author were intriguing and within minutes I was captivated by tales of giant northern Chinamen who kidnapped people and carried them away hidden in clothes trunks.

The next day I decided to explore the environs of Admiralty. It was a very imposing building except for an enormous concrete and brick structure jutting out into The Mall close to Admiralty Arch, not a pretty sight amongst such beautiful architecture, but instinct told me it housed something special. I had been told to report to the Spring Gardens entrance which was located next to the Citadel, which was the name of this inelegant fortress. Satisfied that my map references were correct for the next day, I decided to walk through the Arch into Trafalgar Square to make sure that Nelson and Landseer's lions were still there. I settled down on the steps of the National Gallery with a dried-up Spam sandwich bought from a dilapidated tea shop.

It began to get cold so I walked fast up Haymarket, chilled in mind and body at the spectacle of devastation caused by the bombing. I bought a newspaper from a street stall. The man didn't seem to be doing much trade so I stopped to chat with him. He wore such a worried frown that I felt compelled to ask him what the matter was. He said he was desperately concerned about his elderly mother. Apparently her house in the East End had been bombed, flattened in fact. Her life was saved by firemen who dragged both her and her cat out of the rubble. I thought that sounded like good news, but oh no! he was distressed that, as part of her cellar was still intact she refused to move and had persuaded someone to put a piece of corrugated iron over it to serve as a roof. The cold and discomfort must have been frightful, but she declared that she had been born and brought up in Shoreditch, and in Shoreditch she would stay, Hitler or no Hitler, cat and all. I could understand his dismay, but it did illustrate the tenacity and fortitude of those formidable East Enders. I tried to comfort him without much success.

Another loud explosion from somewhere and the insistent clanging of fire engines sent me scuttling back to the comparative safety of Arlington House. I half expected my fellow Dutch boarders to look more cheerful that evening as my newspaper reported that two days ago the German

Fifteenth Army was in full flight from the southern Netherlands, but alas not a chuckle in sight.

I spent another evening alone wondering about the new job, hoping it would further the encyclopedic intelligence that Ultra provided, and tried to be optimistic that my first penetration into the sanctity of an Admiral's office would not be too taxing. I had timed the walk from the flat to Spring Gardens to the minute and added an extra five to appear keen by arriving early, now there was nothing else to do but eat and go to sleep.

OPERATIONAL INTELLIGENCE CENTRE

On the morning of 3rd November at exactly 0855 hours I presented myself at the unimposing door in Spring Gardens. I had been warned at Bletchley that all hours and shifts were referred to and communicated in naval parlance. You were aboard ship, and shore language was deliberately misunderstood. I presented my pass to a naval steward who stood in a mahogany-lined box just inside the doorway. After careful scrutiny he directed me down a cavernous passage with a decorated marble floor and told me to take the first flight of stairs on the right. I thought the directions were a bit sparse, but that was probably the limit of his knowledge.

On turning right at the first available opening I found the stairs covered in shiny brown linoleum with metal risers. They twisted squarely lower four or five times until I found myself in a narrow passage lit only by fluorescent lighting with the same brown lino on the floor. This must be the Citadel with its forty foot of concrete above. I was impressed despite my nervous churning stomach. You could hear a general buzz of activity and fleeting glimpses of naval officers, W.R.E.N.'s and civilians. I managed to capture one girl, who was on the run with a pile of pink signals, and asked her where I could find N.I.D. 12A. She didn't know; nor did the next three. The fourth, a naval officer, suggested I went down another flight of stairs and he thought it might be halfway down on the left. Good old Bletchley, I thought, even keeping the geography of its office an internal secret.

I found it at last, a brown door with the initials discreetly blurred. I knocked and received no reply, no welcoming "Come in!" I was soon to learn that you never said "come in" within N.I.D. 12A because nobody was allowed in whatever their rank. I waited a minute which seemed like an hour, when the door opened and I was faced with the lovely smiling beam on the features of Annie B., a good friend of mine from B.P. She had disappeared some weeks before from Naval Section and now the mystery was solved. She greeted me enthusiastically and said, "You know the other two of us." She also mentioned they knew I was coming but couldn't tell anybody; nothing new in that! I was then introduced to our boss called Denis, a cheerful picture of a man who resembled a teddy bear. After some words of welcome he explained to me that he only worked day watches and that we four girls would work round the clock in shifts on our own. He operated a system which he assured me made everybody happy; and that the night watch was not as horrific as it seemed.

Working at night had always presented great difficulties to me. The thought of being on my own made me feel very apprehensive, plus the fact that I would be responsible for many unknown factors. I tried to smile spiritedly whilst Denis began to explain the watch procedure. We were to do three day watches and two night watches, with one day off a week. That was generous compared to Bletchley. The timing of the days were 10. a.m. to 6. p.m. and the nights were to be 6. p.m. to 10. a.m. A fourteen-hour night watch might be pretty grim unless there was a lot of work and a "flap" on. I prayed there would be enough to keep me awake in the long, silent and lonely hours.

The welcome and interview over, I now had time to check the surroundings. That was a pretty big word for a very small space. The room was square with two large desks, several filing cabinets and an unaccountable number of telephones, one of which caught my eye immediately because it was bright green and the colour indicated that it was a "scrambler". It was now obvious to me that I had left the junior rankings and would now be able to use such an impressive device. The scrambler telephone was used for carrying on secret conversations between two people. You had to dial the number required, and having got through, you checked it was the person you wished to speak to and made sure they also had a scrambler. After that you then said, "Will you go over?" before you began your conversation. However, I was told with vehemence that scramblers can be decoded and therefore to speak cautiously.

Before Denis began to explain the operational function of N.I.D. 12A (which stood for Naval Intelligence Division) I noticed behind his desk a large wall map with coloured pins stuck into all the warzones. This was to prove very useful because there were four different colours for four girls to identify the positions of their loved ones. Annie B. had already given me a blue one but, until I arrived, she didn't know where to put it. I don't think for a moment it was the map's original intention but we used it for ourselves.

Denis's exposition as to the job left me completely bewildered; but I gathered we were to liaise between Bletchley and Admiralty and all maritime intelligence would filter through the Operational Intelligence Centre in which our small division was situated. Boxes from B.P. would also come straight to us, including a great many communications via the scrambler. This meant receiving naval decrypts from Bletchley and a regular collection of Admiralty signals that might be of interest to the staff at B.P. in the returned boxes. The responsibility for evaluating all this information alone was awesome at first. I began to think that all those dullish days and nights in the Index Room might pay dividends and be of value. I already had a good understanding of decrypts, where they came from and even some quirky habits of the Enigma operators. To simplify it, I had learnt to put two and two together.

After a few day watches under Denis's guidance and tuition, and generous help from the other three girls, I gradually became accustomed to the job and forgot my fears. The boxes appeared regularly, getting fatter every day due to the deciphering speed of Colossus Mark 1 and 2 plus having to fetch the Admiralty signals from Duty Captain's department to be sorted and appraised. It was hard work and I did not dare miss a word from any decrypt; but when the position signals of ships and submarines had to be interpreted with all chart references and coordinates of so many degrees on all points of the compass, I became totally mystified. How on earth was I going to be able to work out that W57.00 by N39.00 was in fact 1,000 miles west of the Azores and that N44.70 by W67.00 was somewhere off the coast of Maine in the United States?

Mercator I was not and Newton's *Principia Mathematica* had not been in my syllabus. This educational lapse was the main source of my worry because, as a result, I was almost numerically dyslexic. Numbers were just a jumble of shapes without any meaning if I had to add them up or, worse, take them away. It had never bothered me before and, when it did I blamed my mother. I had been educated at home by a series of foreign governesses, none of whom I liked and I must have been a truculent student; but they were instructed to ignore mathematics and concentrate on teaching me literature, history, philology and Latin. The latter she thought was the basis of all European languages and would serve me better in life than the integral calculus. She was right in a way. I never had any trouble finding someone to calculate for me. It gave them a feeling of superiority, but it didn't help me find the positions and coordinates of ships. Denis came to my rescue; there was a trick to the solution and he showed me how to do it.

I began to find my way around the catacombs of O.I.C., poking my nose into various rooms, and was amused to find that nobody took any notice of you as long as you had pieces of paper in your hand. I kept clear of Duty Captain's cubby hole on a floor below. He looked rather fierce and I decided to wait until I had something of priority to ask him.

I tested the canteen hopeful that it would provide food less inferior to that at Bletchley. I should have known better for the smell wafted along the basement of Admiralty two corridors away. The word "rancid" sprang to mind; but hunger won the day and I queued up for a plate of fried potatoes, baked beans, a piece of unchewable bacon and a cup of something called coffee with unsweetened condensed milk. It was difficult not to regurgitate the latter because it had the consistency of a wet cowpat. The landlocked navy seemed quite happy with the fare provided, judging from the way they wolfed it down. Perhaps they reflected and compared it to the olden days when sailors caught scurvy from lack of vegetables and had to eat hard tack biscuits with weevils in them. I decided to forego the coffee in future and eat whatever was available; after all, I hadn't exactly sampled haute cuisine during the past four years.

My first night watch was alarming. There I was all alone at 6 p.m. locked up in a small room in the middle of, but utterly isolated from, the rest of Admiralty with a lot of responsibility on my shoulders. Fortunately, it was a very busy night with calls coming in from Bletchley and signals to fetch from the duty watch downstairs which had to be sorted and assessed.

There were several legitimate reasons to use the intoxicating scrambler and before I knew it 10 a.m. had arrived, followed promptly by Denis and Annie's smiling faces. Although our system of night watches and days might have seemed a bit unorthodox it worked to our mutual benefit. Denis was a natural psychologist and he coped most generously with us females. He seemed to understand that we worked under great pressure more frequently than not and sometimes our failings, like splitting headaches, were only human. He knew the total seclusion of N.I.D. 12A was hard at night when nothing was happening to keep us occupied, and that we could not leave the room for very long in case Bletchley became alive. He furtively eased a fold-up camp bed behind the filing cabinets so that, having locked the door, we could catch a bit of sleep in the small hours in between answering the screeching telephones. He also allowed us to change watches or do a double shift if one of our boyfriends happened to be on leave. To my mind he was a bit of a saint.

I have to confess that I remained on night watch rather more than I should have done. The V2s were the main reason. It was horrible sitting in the flat alone with those bloody things crashing down; and the short walk to the safety of the Citadel with its forty foot of concrete above was too tempting to resist. Due to the sobriety and silence of my Dutch friends, it was more fun to share duties with my colleague and pretend to tidy up the office. I was not the only one, however, to use the sanctuary of the Citadel or Lenin's Tomb (as it came to be known). It may have looked like a tomb to some people; but I got to love the old dump and was amused to notice on bad nights the portly figure of the First Lord of the Admiralty prowling the corridors in his bright red silk dragon-patterned dressing gown.

THE DEATH OF *TIRPITZ*

On 12th November 1944 the *Tirpitz*, sister ship of the *Bismarck*, was sunk in Tromsø fjord in Norway by Lancaster bombers from Squadrons No. 9 and 617, who were based at Lossiemouth. This was the moment we had been waiting for because Tromsø was within aircraft range and could now be reached from Scotland. Ultra had reported that several squadrons of German fighters had been moved to an airfield thirty miles from Tromsø, thus giving the mighty ship lethal protection. This must have been just a precautionary decision, because German Intelligence had no idea of the destruction to come.

This enemy air power did not, however, deter the R.A.F. and in all probability they were not told. Luck held, the *Tirpitz* was a naked target to the bomb navigators. The weather had cleared and the protective smoke pots had not been lit because the Germans had not primed them in time. She was hit by at least five huge 12,000 Tallboy armour-piercing bombs dropped from a height of 14,000 feet with uncanny accuracy. Two direct hits had the effect of blowing up the magazine, causing a gigantic explosion; and in her death throes the great ship turned over, imprisoning more than a thousand of her crew in the inverted hull. She lies there still to this day.

She was gone, this mighty battleship which had been the cause of such fear and anxiety. She had kept the ships of our Home Fleet always at readiness in case she decided to leave the Norwegian fjords. Our analyst was proved right. Neither Hitler nor Admiral Dönitz had wanted to risk her against our fleet, despite her superior firepower; and she never made that bid for the open sea. We were overjoyed at this news, euphoric in fact; that menace was now at the bottom of a fjord, never to threaten us again.

Soon after the annihilation of the *Tirpitz*, Admiralty signals informed us that Royal Naval submarines had sunk many Japanese supply ships. Having the previous month decimated several more, the result was a great help to the U.S. Navy in the Pacific. Having almost swept the Atlantic of enemy raiders we were therefore able to send more ships to assist our Allies in the Far East. The American fleet was suffering from the kamikaze suicide pilots. A lot of these planes were shot down but there were always a few who managed to get through to crash on the deck and inflict heavy damage, which in some cases led to the sinking of the ship. These pilots were taught that to die for the Emperor would bring eternal life, somewhere else I presume! But to believe this maxim made them the deadliest of enemies.

It was not all good news though. My generation were devastated by a bulletin that Glenn Miller, on a flight to entertain the troops, was reported missing. This might have seemed a relatively minor loss, but to us it was the end of an era of romance which had sustained us during the war. We had danced and fallen in love to the exquisite music of his band, swaying gently on the dance floor to the rhythm and blues of their strings and percussion instruments. All we had left now were his recordings, which will always touch our hearts and recall magical nights.

By the middle of December I began to know several of the staff in O.I.C. I was not a sailor nor was I a W.R.E.N., I was just a mere civilian from an unknown secret office and tolerated by the friendly mass of gold and navy blue. Most of them I liked and admired for the little I saw of them from the locked and bolted frontiers of N.I.D. 12A. The Senior Service put up with us gallantly, but there is always a last word; for some unknown reason, Admiralty is a civilian organisation.

I much enjoyed my sorties down one flight of stairs, except for the electric cables which ran beneath the passages causing one's feet to draw and sweat. It was a hive of activity, telephones jangling, the click-clack of the W.R.E.N.'s using the teleprinters. Maps and sea charts covered all the available wall space; there were people hurrying in and out changing watches; visiting admirals who regarded you, the civilian, with deepest suspicion; and mysterious V.I.P.'s who might have come from another planet because they always wore a startled expression.

In the large Watch Room the noise was at its loudest with feverish bustle. The duty commanders on watch were never the ogres I had feared but ever helpful, they would answer any question, however irrelevant it might seem to them; and usually, of course, any poser from Hut 4 or Hut 8. The word irrelevant could be classed as an understatement, but they still answered with unfailing courtesy and politeness. This chivalry also extended to dashing young petty officers who would offer to D/F (Direction Finding) you a taxi as you stood shivering with cold at the Spring Gardens entrance after a fourteen-hour night watch.

There was one exception to this rule of honourable behaviour. I suppose there always has to be. This example of nonconformity was one particular signals officer who, when on duty as I fetched the latest batch of Admiralty signals, had a vastly irritating habit of giving me a wolf whistle. This went on for weeks. I tried to squelch his inappropriate volume verbally to no avail. I tried ignoring him but nothing seemed to work. Suddenly I remembered something my godfather, a renowned sailor, told me as a child. Whistling on board was a serious crime because a whistle means a kind of signal or command, such as piping the captain as he boards on or off his ship. It was also used for various other means of communication. This was the end, I was truly fed up and this memory recall was to be my revenge against this obnoxious officer, who obviously thought that all women would fall at his feet.

We met again soon afterwards on the same watch and as I was collecting the usual pink Admiralty signals, there was the same vexatious sound followed by a loud "Wow!" This was the last straw. I dropped the pile of signals in my confusion and rage, picked them up quickly, chronologically all awry, and marched straight into Duty Captain's cubby hole. He looked preoccupied, which was habitual, and asked me what I wanted. I told him I wished to make a complaint against one of his officers. He then enquired what my reason was for this transgression and I replied, "Whistling on board, sir." I had calmed down sufficiently enough by then to detect the glimmer of a smile on his otherwise sober expression and he told me he would severely reprimand the officer concerned for the breach of naval discipline. I had no more trouble after that but hoped the signals officer had not copped too much flak due to my overzealous attitude. Where had my sense of humour gone?

Christmas 1944 passed bleakly because it was so cold. I managed to get forty-eight hours leave to visit my mother on Boxing Day. Her health was a worry and she was on sick leave from the factory. We had been at war for sixty-five months and, although sustained by better news on all fronts, the British were tired but not dispirited. Winston Churchill saw to that; his speeches to the nation were as uplifting as ever and carried us along.

LLOYD'S REGISTER SAVES THE DAY

Although our security was as far as possible superb, there were sometimes curious little incidents where obtaining information bordered on the farcical. One night I was asked by Bletchley to find out the date and departure time from our shores of the S.S. *Queen Mary*, who was acting as a troopship to and fro across the Atlantic. Admiralty didn't seem to have a clue or, if they did, they were not going to tell me. There was one person I did not dare seek help from and that was the director of Naval Intelligence, Commander Denning. He would have told me quite rightly that it was my job to solve the problem and to get on with it. I scuttled down to the Watch Room where the kindly duty captain told me he thought merchant shipping came under the aegis or umbrella of the Ministry of Transport.

Conscious that at any moment Bletchley would be breathing down my neck for the answer (and when B.P. needed information, they wanted it quick and no excuses) there then followed a hilarious hour of handicapped conversation.

I rang the Ministry of Transport, having found the number from the telephone directory. A sleepy voice answered after a while and I asked him if he could "Go over." "Go over where?" he said. It was then that I realised to my consternation that he did not have a scrambler telephone and further more I had a feeling he was the only one there. As the information I needed was naturally Top Secret, this created a huge problem and I had to find a way round it. At 0400 hours after a long night watch it is not easy to think straight, but it occurred to me that if he had a Lloyd's Register of Shipping we could succeed. The question as to whether he had such documentation illustrated the weariness of my mind. So I pinched myself alive and reflected that if the Ministry of Transport did not have a Register of Shipping the world was indeed upside down so I stifled a yawn and gathered my weary wits together. I picked up the telephone again and luckily got the same male voice on the other end. After explaining that I was calling from Admiralty which was Whitehall 9000, extension No. 70, one of our many lines, I proceeded to talk as concisely as possible.

"Have you got that book which begins with the story about a Mr. Edward Lloyd, who had a coffee shop situated in Lower Thames Street, just by the Port of London?" There was a pause at the other end while he digested this strange request. I felt that possibly I could disclose a little more and said:

"I believe he kept a list of ships many years ago for the convenience of traders and seamen." The penny dropped at last. He told me he had that book and, with a certain wry humour, said he found it a jolly good read. I had my copy of the Lloyd's Register of Shipping in front of me, which I had open at the page where the *Queen Mary* was listed. I gave him the page number, said it was one of my favourite passages and would he ring back to confirm his appreciation also?

He returned my call in seconds and by then was not surprised when I gave him the line number on that page. It was now my turn to dial and I was able to ask him the E.T.D. (Estimated Time of Departure) of that particular ship when he returned his call. To his credit, after ten minutes the telephone rang with the information Bletchley required. I passed this on to Naval Section who seemed quite pleased, even mildly startled that I had managed to dig it out so quickly. I breathed a sigh of relief. It had been a struggle, however brief, but, for lack of any other method, I had chosen the right one.

I couldn't help wondering why my employers needed to know exactly when the great ship would depart our shores and cross the Atlantic, which she had done so many times previously. It could not have been the fear of attack by U-boats; she was too fast and zigzagged her way over. I would probably never know, so contented myself with the usual unpalatable breakfast in the canteen.

Towards the end of January, the Russian Army, pushing their way westwards, discovered the extermination camp at Auschwitz in Poland. The horror that met their eyes must have been indescribable. The Nazis had made bungled attempts to cover up the atrocities they had committed by releasing those poor Jewish souls who were still able to walk. Tortured and starved as they had been, it was hard to imagine in their disorientated minds where they would walk to. The S.S. burnt and tried to destroy the gas chambers and the records of their filthy industry, making it impossible for those relatives left alive to join their families. Among the corpses left on the ground were living skeletons, some barely able to move with life ebbing from them. It must have been a shocking and unforgettable sight to witness. It was hellish enough to read about it.

In February Stalin, President Roosevelt and Winston Churchill met together at Yalta on the Black Sea. After winning the war, which now seemed only a matter of time, they made a decision to divide Germany into four zones, each one to be administered by Britain, the United States, Russia and France. Whether this was a good idea or not remained to be seen. It occurred to me that France was in no condition to manage herself let alone a defeated section of Germany. Also we had never completely trusted Stalin and were always mindful that during the last few months that Berlin was his objective and he wanted to get there first.

It must have somehow filtered through to O.I.C. that the four girls in N.I.D. 12A were linguists. As a result there were frequent knocks on our door from naval personnel. They all wanted signals translated as quickly as possible. Most of them were usually from foreign, but not enemy, shipping and contained reports of mine sightings, weather bulletins and positions of ships in various oceans of the world. These signals were not usually of any consequence but you never knew. Something might just knit together with enemy decrypts and, having worked in the Index at B.P., I knew that the importance of even a mundane signal could be paramount.

It was self-evident that we all spoke German and all of us were pretty fluent in French, but the crunch came with Portuguese, Spanish and, horror of horrors, Japanese. Fortunately the latter was naturally classified as enemy transcripts and did not come our way other than the decoded and translated stuff from Bletchley. It became a challenge. Nothing would persuade us that we only had two foreign languages and, by a multiple collection of foreign dictionaries, mostly purloined from the ample library of my great-uncle's flat, we were able to satisfy the enquirer with the English text.

With a basic knowledge of Latin and Greek, from which most European languages are derived, it wasn't so difficult. For instance, if a neutral Portuguese ship signalled the position of a *"dirivida mina,"* it was fairly obvious that it was a floating mine and a prompt reply was forthcoming. I don't think anyone realised that the plenary results were founded on the use of lexicons. This would give us a false prestige, but as long as the job was successful we reckoned it didn't matter.

A FLIRTATION WITH AN ADMIRAL

I had not yet been asked to come face to face with an admiral requesting information. I shivered at the thought, but there was one man I desperately wanted to meet. That was Captain Rodger Winn. R.N.V.R. The promotion to the rank of captain of a reserve naval officer was exceptional, but truly deserved. He was in command of the Submarine Tracking Room and his fame had spread to Bletchley some years before. He had the most uncanny knack of knowing or guessing the positions of enemy submarines during the tormenting months when Bletchley, working flat out, was failing to crack the Shark code. The Tracking Room was my Mecca and I used every possible excuse to visit my hero. It wasn't a very large room and in the centre it had what looked to me like a ping-pong table with a surface of dullish green. This was meant to represent the Atlantic Ocean and on the top were toy reproductions of U-boats placed in different sections. Captain Winn had somehow penetrated the mind of Admiral Dönitz and, with his brilliant reckoning, he had worked out the probable positions of marauding submarines. As soon as Bletchley had completed the struggle, broken the code and said "Jobs up!" the results were astonishing. Rodger Winn's guesswork was correct by all but a few nautical miles. It was little wonder that this man was admired and venerated by all those privy to his work.

I was getting so sick of the canteen food by this time that during day watches I took some Spam sandwiches and an apple to work; and on my lunch break, leaving the benevolent Denis in charge, I scampered across to Trafalgar Square to eat them in the National Gallery. There were wonderful lunchtime concerts on certain days in the Gallery, which was a great joy. Best of all I discovered that on most mornings the organist in St. Martin-in-the-Fields would practice his glorious music. Sitting there usually quite alone in a pew was utter bliss listening to him play Bach's Toccata in Fugue in C Minor. Little did I know at the time that I was to be married in that great church after peace was declared.

Towards the end of March it appeared that Hitler's mental disorder had turned into total insanity. He ordered a "scorched earth" policy, declaring that if Germany lost the war it would no longer be a nation. Everything had to be destroyed, from military installations to railways and food supplies. The news of his psychotic commands and what was left of his reason spread like a tidal wave of exhilaration throughout the offices of O.I.C.

The commission that I had been dreading, namely a confrontation with admirals, finally came one morning from Naval Section at Bletchley. The transmitter had the decency to wish me luck. I had spent many months smiling inanely at any gold braid during my perambulations along the corridors, hoping to be remembered. My orders were to find out the time of departure and the destination of two Royal Naval ships, who were to set forth on some armed intervention. There was no way out, I had to go upstairs and face an admiral, but which admiral? Denis, my boss, chuckled and said he would find out. After a few telephone calls he established that an Admiral Willis might supply the answer, with an emphasis on the "might". The expression on Denis's face, which was full of amusement, made me ask him what was so funny. He tried hard to look serious as he explained to me that this particular admiral was known as Smiler Willis, because he had the reputation of being rather disagreeable, unobliging, suspicious of all intelligence sources and never smiled. Thank you, Mr Birch, you did warn me about the job and I had an instinct that legs would have priority over brains and hoped I was right. As I climbed the brown stairs and arrived on the ground floor paved with smudgy marble my heart began to pound and I felt my stomach flutter. The stewards directed me to the second floor. When I found the right door, I stood outside for a few minutes to recall what my chief in Naval Section had told me: "Use your charm, your legs and your brain." I also felt irritated that Special Intelligence should be treated with disbelief and disdain, which gave me courage.

After my nervous knock I heard the words "Come in" with a sharp authoritative voice. On entry, I found myself facing a lot of gold braid behind a gigantic desk. The admiral looked up from his pile of papers and barked, "What do you want?" With all the moral courage I could muster I replied: "Positions of a Royal Naval cruiser and a destroyer, please sir." I thought he was going to have an apoplectic fit and his face turned a mild shade of purple. He spat out, "Who the hell are you?" I answered as meekly as possible, "N.I.D. 12A, sir." With another bark he said, "And what the bloody hell is that?"

I was getting a bit miffed by that time. To annoy him, which wasn't a good idea, I replied, "Part of Operational Intelligence downstairs, sir." As I suspected, to mention the word "Operational" to a high ranking sailor is tantamount to an insult if he is left sitting behind a desk. Definitely a mistake and I could feel B.P. breathing down my neck. With explosive force further questions were hurled in my direction to which I had to reply, "I'm sorry sir, I cannot tell you." He was so surprised by anyone so junior, and a civilian, answering him with such a blatant refusal that he was temporarily silenced. I realised I was getting nowhere fast and decided that legs had to come into play. I therefore perched myself flirtatiously on the edge of his desk, lifted the hem of my skirt a fraction and proceeded to give him the full treatment.

I told him I had heard so much about him and all his glorious exploits, of which I knew nothing, but he could not have achieved all those beribboned medals and gold braid sitting behind a desk during his naval career. He seemed to melt a little and, when I apologised for taking up his valuable time and being a nuisance, his gruff exterior betrayed a slight twinkle in the eye. With a shrug of his shoulders he said: "I've heard a bit about you lot, come from somewhere in Buckinghamshire have you not? Well I'll give you the information you want, because you have such wanton cheek."

At that point I could have kissed him, but thought that was going too far in our brief courtship. Instead, I stammered my thanks, grabbed my notes and fled downstairs. It was only halfway down that I remembered he had actually smiled. The whole episode proved that Commander Bacon and Frank Birch were right, all the admirals and high rankers needed was contact with another human being, even when they appeared out of the blue with curious questions.

THE LAST FEW MONTHS

Although by now our Allied Forces were now paramount to the Third Reich and it was becoming evident that we would soon win the war, rejoicing was premature because we were bound to suffer further casualties. The German leaders were fanatical enough to spare no mercy to their people and refuse to admit defeat. Martin Bormann, now Hitler's deputy. called upon the exhausted citizens to become "werewolves" or guerrilla fighters to resist the Allies, he said their prayers should be full of hatred and revenge. I could easily imagine that request being treated with disbelief by those poor benighted people.

In April decrypts from Bletchley and Admiralty signals gave us a piece of news which was sorely needed. The most powerful Japanese battleship, the 72,000-ton *Yamato*, was sunk sailing for Okinawa by carrier-based U.S. aircraft. She was apparently on a suicide mission in an attempt to draw off Allied planes from the recent liberation of the island thereby leaving our shipping open to kamikaze attacks. It still astounded me that the Japanese seemed to enjoy obliterating themselves for the sake of their miserable little Emperor.

The 12th of April was a sad day for the Allies. President Roosevelt died. He had been a loyal friend to Britain and a far-sighted man who persuaded the American people to come out of their isolationism and fight the war with us; it must be said that Pearl Harbor helped to change their thinking. He was succeeded by a little man from Missouri called Harry Truman. Nobody over here knew much about him, but he was given the horrific obligation of deciding to drop the atomic bomb on

Hiroshima to finish the Japanese war; a second one was dropped on Nagasaki, because he knew the Japanese would never surrender.

In May 1945 Josef Goebbels fell prey to lunacy. He congratulated Hitler on Roosevelt's death. Perhaps in his folly he thought that it would change the course of the war at the last moment. Wiser Germans, however, reckoned that the President's demise would leave them in the more chilling hands of Churchill and Stalin.

It was in early April when the American forces discovered Buchenwald, a concentration camp like Auschwitz full of the corpses of once fine men. Those that were still alive barely responded to their release; starvation and disease had robbed them of any emotion. It must have been a terrible experience for the battle-weary soldiers unable to help except to pray for the survival of those still living.

There were still in the month of April two more horrors to be exposed; the extermination camps of Belsen and Dachau. I don't suppose there will ever be four place-names so foul in thought and memory in any language the world over. In between these exposures came Hitler's birthday, he was fifty-six years old and we hoped he would celebrate it by listening to the guns of the Soviet Army getting closer and closer to his capital city.

On the 23rd of April the Red Army broke into Berlin from the north, east and south. The next day R.A.F. bombers joined in the near destruction of the city and the whole eastern section was aflame. The German General Wenck made a brave counter-attack from the west, which failed, and Stalin's favourite, Marshal Zhukov, captured the Reichstag, which was the legislative assembly of the Nazi Party. The hated Axis powers were falling apart at breakneck speed, so fast that it was difficult to take in. Was the war nearly over? The phenomenon of our recent successes could hardly be believed after all these years, but our work had to go on, decrypts continued to arrive and the Japanese theatre was still a fearsome threat. On the 28th of April, Benito Mussolini and his mistress Clara Petacci fled Italy towards the Alps, presumably to take refuge in Switzerland, although it was doubtful they would find welcome there even though the country was neutral. He had some fanatical Fascists with him, but he was caught by Italian partisans. They shot Petacci first and then the Duce himself in the chest. These two miserable criminals were then hung upside down in Milan for the people to spit on them; a suitable finale for a strutting egomaniac. An even more fitting end came to the greatest villain of them all. On 30th April Hitler shot himself in his bunker. Eva Braun, his mistress and wife of only thirty-six hours, took poison. Their bodies were carried by Hitler's valet and Martin Bormann up to the garden of the Chancellery, who laid them in a shell hole, doused it with petrol and set fire to it.

Our work did not cease after Hitler's suicide. Goebbels and Himmler were still alive. As a result Bletchley was as busy as usual together with O.I.C. and our office in Admiralty. Naval Section had learned that before Hitler killed himself he had appointed Grand Admiral Dönitz as Führer in his place. As he was the former U-boat commander, he had always been convinced that submarines and only submarines could defeat the Allies. He had created an immense fleet of them and they had sunk millions of tons of our shipping. It would have been vastly more had it not been for Ultra. In early May, as President of the Reich, he moved his government east to Denmark and he was seemingly unaware that quite a few of his U-boat commanders were rogues and might refuse to obey any orders, however, as with General Rommel who was a brilliant soldier, universally admired, like it or not there is no doubt that Dönitz qualified for the same star rating. In Berlin on 1st May there was another ignoble death causing no sorrow to anyone other than a few despotic Nazis that were left. Goebbels poisoned his six young children and then with his wife Magda asked an S.S. soldier to shoot them in the back of the head. A good riddance to a blood-sucking extortionist gauleiter. About the same time Himmler, known as the Jew-baiter, took cyanide to cheat justice. I hope it hurt.

Three days later at a place called Luneburg the German Army in the West surrendered to General Montgomery. His capitulation plans were manifestly severe; his orders were that the troops in the east under the command of Admiral Dönitz were to surrender to the Russians, which must have struck terror into their hearts, but Monty was implacable and the German generals were duly dispatched to General Eisenhower's headquarters at Rheims.

News of victory was gathering apace, but although Dönitz had given orders that all U-boats were to cease hostilities and presumably surrender, as we had predicted many of the submarine captains resented the order and prepared to scuttle or sail to neutral countries. On 5th May the Allied Forces sank five U-boats, including four of the most powerful types on the Kattegat in the Baltic. It was a sensible strike because some of the most voracious Nazis were submarine commanders capable of fighting on alone despite orders. To support this theory, one of the new types of U-boats sank two of our coasters off the Firth of Forth. One point is certain, Dönitz, for all his brilliance, never knew we had been reading his transmissions for five years with the exception of the eight months in 1942 when he suspected quite rightly something was wrong and added the fourth rotor to the Enigma machine. I was on night watch on 7th May, which became known as V. night. I was quite happy about this because in some capricious way I had got used to knowing exactly what was going on and if I didn't know I could find out — it was not in any sense of chauvinism but just a fact of life, that was what Ultra had given me and it would take years to exorcise the enlightenment of Special Intelligence. Of course there were machines of great secrecy even inside Bletchley such as Colossus, the first programmable computer whose speed of decipherment was almost unbelievable. It and future Colossi resided in the Testery in Block F together with the Lorenz cipher machine carrying twelve rotors in binary code. This was Hitler's Geheimschreiber (secret writer) and its code messages were known as Fish. Alas I never saw these magnificent devices, because quite rightly I didn't have the "need to know".

In the early morning of 8th May came the official news of unconditional surrender of the German High Command at Rheims by General Alfred Jodl. The document was signed by General Bedell Smith on behalf of Eisenhower, General Susloparov for Russia and General Sevez for France. Unhappily, the war with Japan continued and we prayed for a swift solution for the Allied Armies still fighting.

I didn't know what to think when I left Admiralty the next morning. The war was finally over in the western hemisphere but at what a cost to service and civilian life. I was too tired to be deliriously joyful and just felt a deep contentment, but as I walked back to the flat along The Mall the sound of church bells began to peal out all over London, releasing the potency of endurance and faith in our victory. We had not heard these bells for five and a half years, the only time they would have rung was in the event of invasion and thank God, unlike the rest of Europe, that never happened. I went back to my flat and fell asleep, too tired to take my clothes off.

That evening I celebrated with friends and met my future husband at a V.E. party, after which we all joined up with the people of London in the streets. Tattered flags were waving, lamp posts were climbed, we cheered and cried with relief all night and remembered those we had lost. It took us a long time to realise peace had come at last.

The next morning, 9th May, I was on day watch and for some very curious reason I was very worried that I now might become expendable. I loved my job with its enormous responsibilities and had grown up with it. I couldn't imagine life without Ultra, much to the chagrin of my fiancé, who was bewildered by my tenacity to stay on at Admiralty now that the war was over, but he was understanding enough not to ask me why and guessed it was something I had to see through.

On arrival at the office, to my great relief Denis greeted me with, "Oh good, you are here, there is a lot going on and I hope you haven't got a V.E. hangover." As we had suspected, several U-boat commanders indignant and resentful of Admiral Dönitz's orders to surrender their vessels had disappeared and if their fuel supplies were sufficient were probably making for South American ports. It was imperative that they should be mopped up and essential that Admiralty should have a comprehensive list of each missing one with number, name of captain and type. This presented a difficulty because they were keeping radio silence and it was patently certain that they would not be using the Enigma codes for there was no one there to receive their transmissions, but their days were numbered. Five U-boats including four XXI were sunk by an Allied airstrike on the Kattegat. U-858, flying the black flag of surrender, steamed into New Jersey, U.S.A. with all her crew standing on deck. As for the other 377 U-boats still at sea, I believe they surrendered. At the end of May it was time to go, the job was practically done and I was very sad, but even sadder when I learnt that Churchill had ordered the W.R.E.N.'s at Bletchley to destroy all the Bombes and the eleven Colossi. I believe one Colossus was allowed to go to G.C.H.Q. but the girls were very upset about all their work over five years liquidated. Perhaps Churchill was frightened of Stalin.

I left Naval Intelligence and N.I.D. 12A in tears.

BLETCHLEY, THANKS FOR THE MEMORY

A NOTE TO THE READER

If you have enjoyed this enough to leave a review on **Amazon** and **Goodreads**, then we would be truly grateful.

Sapere Books is an exciting new publisher of brilliant fiction and popular history.

To find out more about our latest releases and our monthly bargain books visit our website:
saperebooks.com

CPSIA information can be obtained
at www.ICGtesting.com
Printed in the USA
LVHW031025211221
706818LV00005B/578